Once Upon a Curse

Enduring the Everyday Story

Cindy Koch

ISBN 979-8-89043-493-7 (paperback)
ISBN 979-8-89043-494-4 (digital)

Copyright © 2024 by Cindy Koch

All rights reserved. No part of this publication may be reproduced, distributed, or transmitted in any form or by any means, including photocopying, recording, or other electronic or mechanical methods without the prior written permission of the publisher. For permission requests, solicit the publisher via the address below.

Christian Faith Publishing
832 Park Avenue
Meadville, PA 16335
www.christianfaithpublishing.com

Printed in the United States of America

Contents

Foreword by Donavon L. Riley v
Introduction: You Carry the Story ix

Own Your Curse 1
Lies of Freedom 17
Children Are Painful 37
What Is Love? 52
Unearned Thorns 65
More Than You Can Handle 82
Wisdom, Not What You Thought 96
Only One Thing Matters 110
Christ Carried Your Curse Happily Ever After 125

Study Questions 129

Foreword

Once Upon A Curse: Enduring the Everyday Story by Donavon L. Riley

The story that awaits the reader in what follows will challenge their perceptions, shatter illusions, and invite them to think deeply about the profound truths that are examined within the pages of "Once Upon A Curse."

In this remarkable book, author Cindy Koch delves into the depths of the curse that has plagued humanity since the dawn of time. It is a curse that reverberates both within the sinful, dying world that surrounds us and within the recesses of our own hearts. From the very first pages, we are confronted with the stark reality of our existence, exposing the rawness of our darkest desires and the intricate web of lies that entangles our quest for freedom.

"Once Upon A Curse" fearlessly examines the multifaceted aspects of this curse, casting a discerning eye upon the pains and challenges that arise within our relationships, particularly with our children. No stone is left unturned as the author fearlessly navigates the treacherous waters of misunderstood love, unfulfilled expectations, and the haunting specter of depression that accompanies a life derailed from its intended course.

But this isn't meant to scare us away, because within these pages lies not only the stark portrayal of our shared human struggle but also the blazing light of Gospel hope God uses to pierce through the darkness. Through an unflinching exploration of the curse's consequences, we are compelled to confront our own mortality, the depths of our isolation, and the illusions of false wisdom. It is within these crucibles that God reveals to us the very essence of our existence, stripping us down to our core, exposing the urgency of our need for salvation.

With each turn of the page, we come to understand that God does not invite us to embark on a journey of self-discovery, but rather forces to face the realities that plague us all. In his faithful, loving-kindness God makes us embrace the weight of our curse so that, ultimately, we may receive the profound solace of his promised forgiveness and mercy revealed to us through Jesus Christ. In the resolution of our sin through the salvation of Jesus Christ proclaimed to us for the forgiveness of sin, we find the key that unlocks the path towards a happily ever after, where the burdens of our curse are lifted and redemption becomes an irrevocable reality.

So, prepare yourself for a unique fusion of perspectives, where the passion of a wife and mother, the profound theological insights of a baptized sinner, and the unyielding fearlessness of a literary maverick converge into a singular voice that will challenge, inspire, and ignite the reader's excitement for the Gospel of Jesus Christ. Open these pages and discover the extraordinary power of "Once Upon A Curse" - a book that will forever change the way you perceive your own story.

And don't be afraid to embrace the truth about our shared curse, dear reader, because it is in facing it that we discover the true beauty of our redemption. So, may your heart be stirred, your mind be expanded, and may the Holy Spirit set your imagination ablaze as you delve into the extraordinary narrative that awaits within these pages.

ONCE UPON A CURSE

Welcome to a book that reveals the truth about our shared human experience, where God transforms curses into blessings and where, against all odds, a happily ever after awaits sinners in the loving embrace of our Lord and Savior, Jesus Christ.

Introduction

You Carry the Story

The dream of once upon a time is the proper beginning of any story, as the fairy tales tell us. You also have grown up since childhood listening, loving, and believing certain stories that have been told you have lived once upon a time. But is it a proper beginning to your story, or to my story—once upon a time, a unique story, just once upon a single, unreproducible time?

My story is the most typical of any. I had two parents, two siblings, and a normal home life. We went to school, my parents paid their taxes, and no one had to break out of a mental institution. Every Sunday morning, we tried to go to church, sang the songs, drank the coffee, and usually skipped out on Sunday school. "Well rounded, adjusted"—that's what my school counselor wrote on my high school report card.

I grew into my own family, children, church, education, and homemade chicken and rice casserole. It was comfortably undifferent. And the stories of once upon a time had no bearing on my life. It was about surviving this time, enduring this place, raising the children, making it one more day. We were the only people in our small, little world because that is all we could handle.

But the babies grew, the world was opened to them, to me, to the possibilities that lay outside of my window. The stories, the people, the experiences—as different as we were, I only began to see how many of us shared the same story. Even though the same story was told in a million different ways, I still held on to the belief that my story, my family, and my experience were completely unique.

Taught by modern independence, each special "once upon a time" is an attractive storyline, for everyone carries a story, an exclusive timeline and stage of events that have shaped you into who you are at this moment. Some stories, you have been an active part of; some have been shaping and molding you against your will. Some have been victorious, and some have been soul crushing. But you know where you have been. You carry your story with you.

Because of this intimate connection to your own story, you may believe that this experience is completely your own. There is comfort and validation in the inner self, rather than just part of a community identity. Deep inside, wisdom and knowledge have been taught to you from the depths of your own experience.

Yet as unique as you are, there are stories that you also share with others. Spanning time and distance, region and language, we exist together in a tangible world. By the logic of history, there has been a beginning and will be an end to our human journey, as disjointed as it all specifically may seem. There is an overarching narrative that not only speaks about you and your past but prepares your future and the future of those to come after you. You have been adorned, dressed for your journey, whether you know it or not.

You carry a story.

But this story is more than just a chapter or two that hangs together loosely and with an unexpected twist. This is a deep story that roots in our identity, the most basic piece of who we are. Decisions are based on our identity. Habits are formed from our identity. Goals are created out of our identity. What we do in everyday life is a manifestation of who we believe that we are. And so there is a foundational story we must expose.

A popular misunderstanding is that you are free to mold and form yourself from scratch. You are free to decide your identity, be it a peace officer or a butterfly. Rather, we will learn that there is a huge part of our unchangeable identity revealed to us in the story that we carry. Our decisions can only go so far. Our individual paths only last for so long. Still we hold on to the hope that we are each the creator of our own lives and existence. We misunderstand the need for an outside voice of authority. We take great offense to another story that may change our identity. But there is a greater story that we will recognize in our lives and in the lives of others.

In the chapters to come, the chaos of our individual stories will meet the collective. Hers and his, yours and mine, simple and complicated—everyday struggle will crash into objective truths. You may recognize your own tales, and you may not. But it is too easy to get lost, as they say, in the detailed trees of your subjective experience. Although, the opposite problem exists when you get lost in the philosophical ideas of the forest. But in fact, the story that you carry is both personal emotions and impersonal reactions replaying the beloved scenarios of history. And all of this relates to a great metanarrative preserved outside of us. You carry your personal story but also the story of the entire creation. Your participation in this world of love and triumph and heartache and failure ultimately connects you to those walking next to you.

Amid these short narratives in the next chapters, you are challenged to carry your own story, both great and small. Your story is yours alone, but do not forget that you also carry along the stories in the following pages. Consider how you bear these same burdens. What if you also live "once upon a curse"?

We are not lonely nor disconnected, as different as our experiences may be. But the way in which you realize relationship may be shocking. You expect friendship in your victories, in your good times, and in your glories. But it is necessary that you find community in another place, disobedience and suffering, exposing your weakness, admitting your falsehood, and receiving the story and your identity in a vulnerable way. And by this, you may suddenly recognize those who are struggling beside you, who also share the same story.

The short stories of individual people sketched in the following pages only add a slice to the big picture. They are tiny snapshots with no beginning and no grand finale, because personal stories are not beginnings nor ends in themselves. Rather, each scene points toward the grand narrative in which we all live and, in some sense, with which we have all been burdened. Our minuscule stories all point to a universal beginning and to the greater end that encompasses all creation.

Your greater story begins at the start of the world. God's Word tells us in Genesis that God created the heavens and the earth. Yet it is only good for a few short days. God's human creations played out their very own story, not the story given to them. In the beginning, rather, man and woman lived their own small piece of a story, disobeying the One who created it all. So God proclaimed curses on His perfect creation. God spoke about how the world must work differently now that it was changed by sin, a story that God did not intend. Speaking these curses to the serpent, to the first woman, to the first man, God spelled out the reality of our newly tainted creation. It has become less than what God made it to be.

This book seeks to interpret our tiny experience in light of the greater story of perfection lost. This book invites you to see that our world was not only changed by the first people who went against the Almighty God. Rather, as you already know, it is a changed existence for your story and for mine as well.

Even if you can admit this, that you are a participant in a greater story beyond the scope of your limited vision, there is another mountain on the horizon, that the outcome of this story is far beyond your control. This broken world is overtaken by evil hearts and hands. You cannot fix it, as much as you want to. There will still be depression, lack, pain, and death. Even the simple pieces of life you think to have under control, there is still a brother or sister that is being crushed. The past, present, and future will surely include obstacles and unhappy chapters. By no choice of your own, this is unavoidable.

And our inclination is that a "once upon a time" should be a happy story for us, beginning to end. But my friends, that is the absolute beauty of our tragedy. Sadness and pain are not our whole story. The curse and our unfulfilled longings instead face us directly toward the cross of Christ alone.

It is not enough to expose that you are not able to carry your own story. For everyone, the failing of this world is too much to bear. However, the confrontation of "once upon a curse" will challenge to remind you who you really are. You will recognize the identity given to you, not only by the hardships we all endure but also by the promises of Jesus's death and resurrection for you. Finally, there is an answer. Your essential Savior has ended the curse under which we all struggle. And every piece of your story is completely finished for you.

Own Your Curse

I have always wondered about the stories of those who appear to have it all figured out. Stages are set as if there is nothing to hide. Cameras are poised at the best angle in the best light. Actors present themselves as if there is nothing to fear. Yet we instinctively know that it is much harder to live in a world that is wracked with problems. Quickly, though, we become exhausted from stories that cannot admit these unanswerable twists of life. Are the false storylines saving you, dear reader, from our broken world? Did the neat and tidy quips of wisdom provide an escape from your darkest fears and desires? No, an ignorantly joyful path doesn't save us from ourselves, nor should it distract us from the enduring answer.

If we can put ourselves in the hearts and minds of others, who are also seeking to answer their own unanswerable questions, we finally understand that we are not alone. Our problems are deep. But more importantly, we all must own that truth, not avoid it. God calls out loud, "Where are you?" And we just can't hide by ourselves anymore. Strangely enough, our honest exposure will become the pathway to the answer. Every one of us needs a hope that finally solves our issues rooted in the curses, and we may need each other to see it.

*****

Like the crack of a gunshot across another blank, quiet morning, that hollow mechanical pulse snapped her awake. Because there was no other sound to mask the shock of the ordinary, the click before the alarm, the alarm was again set for nothing.

Involuntary heart pumping with a fight or flight purpose, the alarm clock felt like the most excitement Jen has had in ages, until she realized it was, in fact, the most excitement she has had, about three months to the day. Awake and asleep with the purposelessness of the morning recalled, she stared into the too-bright sunlight through a tear in her crooked blackout shade. Why did she even set the alarm anymore? Was it a faraway hope that today would be different?

This new reality of nothing in the mornings and nothing in the afternoons felt like a dream from which she couldn't awake. Before, her life was scheduled to the minute. Before, there were plenty of goals, challenges, and passions to focus her attention. Before, she was a successful and productive human being. Before, the whole world was locked down, hiding, in a holding pattern, at home.

Her daily conversation had evolved into something like this: "Get up. You can't stay in bed all day. Well, why not? What am I going to do when I get out of bed? I can't go anywhere. I don't have any emails to answer or any work that is breathing down my neck. But you can't just sleep your life away. You need to find something to do, or else you're going to just give up and die in this bed. Well, I do have to pee, so that's something."

Quiet apartment. Blank calendar. Stale city. Jen brushed her hair over the sink. The mirror showed bruised circles under her eyes, although she had more sleep now than ever in her life. Maybe it was just the shock of her bare skin—unmade, untouched by cosmetics for at least a week. Dead-shaded lips. Did she really look that old now? Without all the fillers, the smoothers, and the colors, this may be a more real Jennifer than she had ever been bold enough to see.

Jennifer—that was only what her mom called her. She hated that name. Constantly compared, never enough, failure of a girl looking back in the mirror, she tried to ignore those thoughts and memories. It was easy to do before. But today, more and more, she was viewing the disappointment that her mother must have always seen.

Brushing, brushing, watching, thinking to fill the quiet. What should she do next? What could she do next? Get dressed, or stay in her stretch pajama pants. No one cares. No one is looking for her. But even her softest llama flannel PJs feel different than they used to. Previously welcomed after a long day of heels and tight straps on pants or panties or bras or shoulder seams, three months ago, when pajamas become her everyday attire, they itched like absence. Their comfort melted into soft shackles, and she tried to deny that she is becoming indifferent to escape.

Today, however, Jen wasn't strong enough to come up with another lie with another artificially constructed reason. She thought she had figured out a pathway through this life. She thought that things were only going to get better the older and wiser she becomes. That was before. Lately, however, she had to consider that she lived in a world that was out of her control. She never saw it quite like that before.

So she lay down again, catching up on the "news" on Instagram and her "friends" on Facebook. Maybe death wasn't the worst thing ever. Eternal sleeping is all she did nowadays. Head slammed on a pillow just to hear some kind of sound, reaching over to the offensively bright digital clock, this time, Jen turned off the alarm so it would no longer interrupt her.

Scroll.

Yawn.

Blank.

She jolted back awake. How long had she been asleep this time? Screaming blurry voices shocked Jen's eyes open. It was from the next-door neighbors.

"I hate you!"

Shrieking and crying muffled, at first she thought it was the tail end of an unresolved dream. Shouting, crying, unable to recognize the dirty particulars, slurred-together speech from sobs and distance. Sprinkled with raw profanity, painting the pain with the ever-rising volume of a family disturbance. Suffocated by thick striped wallpaper in a sensible neutral color. These walls were pretty thin, and she knew more about this volatile family recently than she ever cared to know.

"You don't appreciate." "You don't pay attention." "You don't even care." "You don't respect." "I don't want to be here." "You—I don't even like you." "What did I do with my life?" "Why am I still here right now?"

Back and forth, high-pitched darts were wildly thrown. It was too much to bear. Too much silence? Too much noise? They had to release the tension. Through her wall, she was imagining the tears streaming down her face, gurgling under her breath. Rage was burning the lining of her stomach. Flushed cheeks and stressed, wrinkly skin, from her comfortable bedroom coffin, Jen longed to feel something intense, like what she could only hear from the apartment next door.

Locked inside, she was alone. They were trapped together. A sweet, simple truth climaxed among slams and screams. A sentence violently cried along in harmony from her own silent soul. The spirit of angst flowed freely through the apartment complex. Jen could have sung along.

"I feel like a failure!"

Sympathetic to the sobs, Jen exhaled the heavy air unconsciously held in her own dark belly. Every bit of their body and soul convulsed at each other next-door, out loud against the injustice of the universe. Every bit of her own body and soul shriveled under the sweaty comforter, all alone.

Only feet away from her solitude, the neighbor mother and daughter pushed each other over the edge by a word, a look, an absence of understanding. These are the moments of unfiltered emotion, where the little things finally ignite into destruction. Tonight, the entire apartment of quarantined strangers had an opportunity to participate in the drama. It was a public invitation for all to dredge up their very same angst, disillusion, discontent, and failure.

*****

Isolated and together, too little and too much at the same time, highlighting the rifts and ridges, drawing attention that we disappoint each other in thought, word, and deed. These are the failures we try to avoid because everything should be fine, not just for a girl stuck in a quiet apartment, for a family trapped next door, or for each of us who feel the missing pieces of the beauty in life we desire. Sometimes, we have seen behind the curtain, and these are realities we want to ignore and explain away until we cannot ignore it anymore.

Suddenly trapped, we all end up here at one time or another. Whether it was for actions and life events that we could control or the situations we suddenly awoke to, things that are entirely not our fault. It's not just fine. And the future might not turn out for the better. Questions, emotions, memories, shame, misunderstandings, anger, and disappointment come into focus in the darkest of times, especially when everything else goes quiet.

When there is a hush in the external noise, we are exposed in the moment to reflect on our paths and choices. Loneliness may define and overtake. Husbands and wives may drift together or farther apart. Children may learn that their world is an unforgiving and unstable place. The put-together, perfect American dream may shimmer like smoke, even if just for a second. Sometimes, we accidentally notice the monsters that have always been living under our beds, in our heads, or on the other side of the dinner table.

Yet this era is not the only one that has felt desolate pain. We are not the only ones who have heard the angry screams next door. Generations have hidden from the nothingness day after day. And yet the destructive reality we take part in always renders shock once we realize that the world is legitimately falling apart. Our lives are still broken, even after all of these years of self-help apps, enlightened philosophies, and parenting books.

One fine day, you may be brave enough to admit that you are no better than those who went before you. The life you thought was made better, the future you thought had been built—a long-time truth smashes into what we see in our cultivated jobs, leisure, and prodigies. Finally, one day, you may discover; this world is miserable.

Your children are terrible. You are on the wrong path. One day, you may be bold enough to the question: What did I do wrong? What is the problem with everything I have known up to this point?

I was told as a little girl that I could write my own story and create my own life. To some extent, that may have been true. I made choices that directed my particular steps in one way or another. I have written my way into a unique experience that you do not have. You also have particular twists and turns on your own path that I will never know. But our story began before we did. We live in a world that was here before we were, and it will be here after we are gone.

Perhaps you were under the spell of control and meaningfulness for a while: that you could change the world, that you were plotting the path to the greatest kingdom on the earth. In such a short disillusionary time, you bind yourself to incredible lies of expectation. But when reminded of this uncontrollable world full of sick and dying people, including ourselves; full of bondage and slavery, including our own, despair takes over. A good, hard look at society, at the freaked-out reactions, at your inconclusive and divisive answers that don't answer anything—you conclude something is not right. Something is out of control, out of reach, in a world actively trying to infect us, reaching out to suffocate us at every turn, whether it be our business, our free speech, the opportunities for our children, or even our very own physical bodies. You thought you did it differently; it didn't matter. You thought you were on the right path, and it leads to death and destruction. Hope for a better tomorrow suddenly slips through your fingers. Your children will not have the answers either. It was an artificial daydream that you could outrun this cosmic curse on humankind, on this creation. Reflection reveals that it is not getting any better down here. This is nothing new.

Not only is the story bigger than us, but it also is not a unique story. Consult the unabridged history books to see wars and rumors of wars, pandemics and plagues, severe moral failings, and empire collapses. Our generation has not been experiencing anything that is new under the sun, even if every disappointment and failure is an unprecedented experience in our own lives. In fact, what is more unusual might be our unchallenged prosperity, safety, and comfort in perpetually hostile territory. Glory, honor, and fame are not the best reminder that we are not in ultimate control.

You are not the creator of this reality. You have been part of a story that has lasted a very long time. You are not the almighty storyteller of all time and space. You are the characters and creations of such a world and an already-existent story. Your ability to control the story is nothing more than a misguided dream. Ignorance of the truth keeps you from taking comfort in what is real. Incomprehension of your place in the world leads to trust in lies, self-knowledge, freedom, and other made-up fables. So while a slumber may be easier, especially in the face of disappointment and pain, the truth will absolutely set you free.

If you dared to confess that you are not the author and perfecter of your reality, you will become aware of an ancient, hidden wisdom. Where you exist, in the middle of an incredible story, there were those who came before you, and there are those who will come after. With any great adventure, the beginning is essential for a journey to the end. And you never flip to the center of that juicy novel, of course. It would do an injustice to begin in the middle. You don't simply infer what has happened according to how you think the story should have started. Instead, you enjoy the beginning, listen to the story that is told, and eventually find yourself in the middle of it.

And so this story calls for a particular type of honesty about disappointment, honesty about despair, honesty about your failures, honesty about this crumbling and dying world, honesty that hurts, honesty about your place in the greater collective history, honestly searching for a solution in this world where you have all found yourself both trapped and liberated.

Honesty prepares you for knowledge of the beginning of our story. It has been told again and again from generation to generation. In fact, this is one of the most often-told stories on the planet. But it's not just popular; there is more internal and external evidence for the truth of this than most of the historical facts that our world unquestionably believes. Even among the thousands of individual manuscripts recounting this story, it was written by a true authority. The ultimate storyteller is the one who created the earth and sea and sky. He speaks, and it is so. His word is creative and does incredible things. The storyteller said, "Let there be light," and it actually happened. At the beginning of every story on this planet, the storyteller was present before everything and will be there after everything ends. He has written your story, my story, the same story of those who are not yet ready to confess this truth.

God breathed life into dust, filling raw lungs and heart and mind with the light of life. He created the very first person and broke him in two. From a sliver of a man's side, He built another. Breath and heart and mind, they, both man and woman, were formed as His beautiful people. And He was their God, their Creator, the first storyteller.

This story, this world, this reality, is a Garden full of every kind of good thing. His people had every provision that they needed, everything that they wanted. It was enough to sustain them forever. They had a Heavenly Father that was pleased with their word, action, and deeds. They were the most honored beings among His entire creation.

Yet, as the story goes, there was a single tree from which they were not allowed to take, not allowed to eat, not allowed to enjoy—a tree of knowledge, a fruit that would open their eyes to good and evil. This was the one thing that God kept from them. This was the taste that would close their eyes to God's reality. And as the story unfolds, this wisdom is the one thing they ended up wanting the most.

In the cool, misty Garden of Eden, woman couldn't stop looking at that sparkling fruit. Feeling the hunger welling up on the tip of her tongue, she thought, *What would that taste like, that unknown fruit, that dangled between the leaves?* And to enflame her curiosity, a word from the serpent sang her to consider sleep. Sun and fresh air, intoxicating freedom. One afternoon, she felt an inspiring whiff of unexplored possibility. The thought of it tingled somewhere too deep to recognize. Built for exploration, creation, and movement, how could she just stay still? There was a whole world out there to experience, to touch, to taste.

What if? Who said? What did God really say? Her own imaginative pen moved too quickly.

The woman didn't want to be spoken for, to have a story written for her. Really, she did everything to avoid that. She didn't want to default to someone telling her what to do, to someone telling her what was true. She desperately wanted to write a story, one she could call her own, one of her own creation before she ever knew what was happening. So she just began creating for herself as she closed her eyes, shut her ears, and fell into the darkness.

It turned out not to be her story alone.

Hidden and shaded, scratching bushes and new-felt shame, both man and woman found themselves bound in a prison that they never imagined—alone, together, and scared. They were lonely, side by side, and sick, hiding in the bushes from the Almighty Creator. *What did they do?* Random or deserved, they were found in the middle of consequence.

They listened to the beating of their own heart instead of the Word from the one who wrote this story for them, God. At this point, His great story feigned a false beginning. One was born from a mortal heart and mind instead of an eternal story that God was already telling. They, the first beloved people, took and ate. They did change the world. Without even knowing it, the consequences were devastating. The eternal story of gift and truth drifted into a tale of incredible rebellion.

The consequences impacted not only Adam and Eve but the entire earth, their children, and ours as well. Man, woman, and child still drown in the residual pain from their decision. We all have ended up lost and confused and exist somewhere in the middle.

Yet, just like Adam and Eve, we also misunderstand with sleepy eyes and closed ears. The lie we like to believe is that our great story originates somewhere inside of us, that we are the director of its outcome, that we can control the world, that we are not living in the middle of a story that already encompasses us, teaches us, and is a part of our every day.

It is painful and humiliating to admit that we are inside this story—an unknown story, an inescapable story, an unfair story. Yet the foundational beginning of the most important story that we will have to learn in our lifetime is that we are not the storyteller. This is not our personally created story, but we are a piece of it. Generation after generation, we all struggle to understand what the part is that we actually play.

God does not leave His people alone to believe their handmade lies, not in the Garden in the beginning, not in the confusion of our own stories. He is there when we want it or even when we don't. And He is there in both condemnation and salvation.

"Where are you?" asked the all-knowing author. He knew what man and woman had done. They ate the fruit, spurned the gift, made a fool out of everything that was good and given. Even though the couple was hiding in their filth, He knew exactly where they were and what they had done. They disobeyed their Creator and Maker, even though He had clearly spelled out the punishment. And these are the consequences—an altered reality, curses, and death.

He speaks. It is written. And it is so. To the deceiving serpent, who was cast as the villain:

> Because you have done this,
> cursed are you above all livestock
> and above all beasts of the field;
> on your belly you shall go,
> and dust you shall eat
> all the days of your life.
> To the woman he said,
> "I will surely multiply your pain in childbearing;
> in pain you shall bring forth children.
> Your desire shall be contrary to your husband,
> but he shall rule over you."
> And to Adam he said,
> "Because you have listened to the voice of your wife
> and have eaten of the tree
> of which I commanded you,
> 'You shall not eat of it,'
> cursed is the ground because of you;
> in pain you shall eat of it all the days of your life
> thorns and thistles it shall bring forth for you;

> and you shall eat the plants of the field.
> By the sweat of your face
> you shall eat bread,
> till you return to the ground,
> for out of it you were taken;
> for you are dust,
> and to dust you shall return. (Genesis 3:14–19)

Cursed is the land. Cursed is the story. These consequences from the storyteller changed the course of your world.

Immediately, the beautifully and wonderfully made serpent's feet disappear. He was created to love and serve God. He was created to be cared for by the man and woman, like any other animal. But, now, in a world of curses, the very freedom to run away and go where he pleases is taken back from him. He is changed as cast on his belly onto the ground. Once breathing in the fragrant berries and flowers made for eternal enjoyment, his lips and nose now pressed into the dank dust, mildewed coughing sludge, now forever tasting the grime of existence because he overtook the story that was not his.

But not only the serpent ate creation's leftover dirt; all the animals, birds, trees, mountains, rivers, families, and individual stories tasted dust. Not only was the serpent's body changed, but every experience with a harmonious meaningful productive world has lost its legs as well. This is the consequence in the beginning, in the tragedy of your greater story.

All generations have been born from this story. And we all have tasted it. That it is not quite right. We imagine a world that could be better. We tell ourselves that we can strive for that better, perfect thing to make it so, to write our own middle while living in the midst of it. But honestly consider, dear reader, you may not have the power that you think you do. You may find yourself written into this cursed reality.

These curses set in motion the heartbreakingly hard story that you must live right now. You have been so rearranged from creation that you actively choose to do the evil thing. And it feels like exactly what you want to do. This is the story, that you can't even choose the right path. There is no one righteous, not even one. When the storyteller, who created and spoke the world, gave every good thing, He also told you who you are. You may be grasping for meaning, struggling to understand. You may be continually unhappy, trying to make it all right. But when the storyteller who created and spoke the world gives every good thing, He also tells you who you are. He tells you, and you are not the author. In fact, you have sinned and fallen short of the glory of God. This is an entirely different starting point, that you are not the creator of what is good and right and faithful. Rather, you are caught in the middle of what already is, that you are sinful, broken, living with curses, and less than what you were made to be.

But our helplessness is the beginning of the answer, not in avoidance, not in solution but in the simple understanding of the gravity of this situation.

The increasing weight of helplessness crushes a spirit. Admitting the depravity of heart and soul and mind, admitting the ineffectiveness of action and will, admitting that you cannot change the greater outcome of this sad story—this honesty will drive you to despair. Unfortunately, most happy Instagram influencers will not be ready to take such a leap. But there is no lasting answer that you can construct. There is no enduring world you can build. Eventually, there is no escaping such a real and devastating realization that you, I, we live in the midst of God's curse.

This does not just pertain to us, our children, and our grandparents, but this message is for everyone who has had to walk away from the Garden of Eden. A cursed wilderness is where we dwell. This is the story that you were born into, long before you ever made one little decision in your own life. This is the story that you will not be able to change, not be able to do over or fix, not be able to go back and restart the story. It is vitally important to see it, to feel it, to recognize the reality of our dying creation. Remember where you wander. Remember that there are problems that you cannot solve, no matter how good or clever you become. The curses remain, and you cannot reverse them. Yet there is an answer.

Pride and know-it-all righteousness will only fool you into complacency. Because if you see clearly, if you speak honestly, if you know this story, there is much you cannot achieve in this world and in this lifetime. This is the great secret of the ages, the foundation of all wisdom. You are not okay. You are not fine. This world is not right. You see your failures. You see your indecision. You see your culpability should you ever be held accountable. You should regret your haughty pride. You should be ashamed that you ever thought you could outsmart, outlive, outlove.

If you desire, try it. I dare you. Change the world, and be disappointed that nothing endures. Try it. Expect greatness, and find failure. Attempt to beat death, and you will eventually die. It's thoroughly depressing. It's incredibly scary because this is the reality that you are trapped in today. You are not free to choose your own adventure. Yet exposing the curses in our world, in this life, in ourselves is painful, absolutely. At the same time, exposing the curses is a great gift of wisdom. Remembering the blessed beginning, you will be enlightened in the fearful middle. But the end is still to be fully realized. Today or yesterday or tomorrow, there is a story of salvation that becomes clear to those who struggle with the lack.

> The fear of the Lord is the beginning of knowledge. (Proverbs 1:7)

Fear is the beginning of knowledge, especially when we must admit that we cannot save ourselves. The best of us lack all conviction, while the worst of us are full of passionate intensity. And the best of us haven't lacked quite enough in this lifetime, yet the worst of us know what it feels like to have it all stripped away. And the worst of us then have been prepared to hope for something beyond these curses. It has already been spoken, and there is nothing you can do to speed the healing of this world or the healing of your own body and soul. The only thing left to do is fear. Fear your knowledge. Fear your place in this creation. Fear yourself. Fear is the beginning, if you are strong enough to learn the truth.

Once upon another time and place, a disillusioned boy found himself lacking. He was starving, not like he used to say when it was four in the afternoon in front of a fully stocked pantry. He was pit-of-the-stomach hungry. He had gone three nights now without something solid to eat. It was barely enough to simply keep him alive under a tree by the river because at least there was water. He remembered the days of working with his brother, long days in the hot hilly sun. You have to have water. That wide open sky of windy memories, brother, father, fire smoke, hot pot of soup—those were the satiated moments he tried to forget every black night, hiding under his stolen blanket.

He finally was afraid for his life. The unforgiving world had, at last, offered him the truth, shivering, outside and dark, trying not to remember his bed, fresh clothes, soft pillow. Back then, he would feel rested; he would feel full; he would feel that everything was okay, in pieces. He had the chance now to remember the perfectly moderate temperature of his childhood bedroom, unlike the freezing temperatures of this night. Tonight he struggled to ignore the savage pig snorts and grunts inches away from his ear. Tonight he unconsciously gripped his knife a little tighter in fear, shivering beneath under his ragged, worn quilt.

Father, back home, had his ideas. At the time, they were intolerable. Work, give, go, do—the prodigal boy had his own ideas. He had more to discover and other paths to take. He was unsatisfied with the work given to him. He was lost in meaningless skepticism by the story his father kept trying to make him believe. He thought there should be more to this life. So long ago, not long ago at all, he had taken his inheritance and left.

But tonight, this boy dared to wonder about his greater story in this cursed world, whether it was set in the safety of his home or here in the middle of the wilderness. Just as unsatisfying was the work he did not have. Just as meaningless was this world where he had nothing to give. Just as disappointing were the ugly scarred-up women, pretending that they were young and beautiful seductresses. It turned out, he had nowhere to go and nowhere else to run. He was just as trapped on the outside as he was on the inside.

This boy, dared to be honest. He dared to admit the truth about the world around him. It was no better. In prosperity and health, in poverty and sickness—he was drowning in the mud of a curse, as was the unfaithful world where he failed to find a job. For the first time, he feared. He confessed that his story was greater than him alone. His indignation did not solve the problems he wished to escape. His short-term solutions did not change the outcome of this sad reality. By this cruel knowledge, the boy awakened a man.

He returned home to his Father, relying only on the grace and mercy that had always been there. Finally, he could see the end as he found strength in the story that had been told to him. He was free to expect reconciliation in the despair and trusted external salvation in the midst of the dark world that surrounded.

> The fear of the Lord is the beginning of knowledge. (Proverbs 1:7)

And if you can admit the fear of the Lord and the reality of the incontrollable curses, then you also are prepared to receive the truth. Whether you are a lonely, exhausted, suffering, woman, man, boy, or father, the fear of the Lord and the humility of our need is knowledge about the world, about our God. It is the realization that we must depend on His mercy. He is the only One that can overcome the monumental shift in His own story.

God does not leave His people alone. Even from the first failure, He asked, "Where are you?" The all-knowing author knows what has been done to His creation. The storyteller foreshadows your incredible resolution when the curses were first spoken to man and woman. The head of the original deceiver will be crushed, and the world will be set right again. The gracious decision of a God who created all things will endure, not these curses. A Savior will be given for you, and He alone will restore the world. He is for you in the midst of these curses, revealing His action of salvation.

Own your curse. This honesty clarifies a hope outside of yourself. But also understand, it is not your whole story. Own your curse, and you will hunger and thirst for the true answer. Own your curse so that you cling to the promised end of rest and restoration. Remember that your fear, the admission, the truth, is only the beginning of your true and everlasting solution.

Lies of Freedom

The illusion of freedom is the most prestigious fable told to mankind. A lying serpent taught the wide-eyed woman in the Garden of Eden that she was free to choose her own path outside of the will of the Almighty God. Once upon a time, this first human believed she was totally free. But she quickly discovered that this was not true by the curses from God.

Since then, these curses have been etched into our interaction with this world, originating in that first lie of the devil. Not only externally, but lies of freedom also plague the depths of our own hopes and desires. From the very beginning, we have been tricked into believing that the answers are found in our freedom of choice. However, over and over again, our story of struggle with Satan is answered by true freedom through God's Son.

*****

Only in the truck did Nick feel free. Settling into that worn leather seat was like stepping into another world, controlled environment, plenty of room for his legs to stretch, just enough. No one, without his permission, could enter. A familiar resting place for his hands, purpose driving him forward. The wilderness, tamed and conquered, strapped and tethered to the trailer, tied up under his power, now subject to his rule. Unable to touch him, unable to reach him, safely secured in the rearview mirror, here on the driver's throne, in another dimension, Nick exhaled a breath of relief.

He had turned off the radio years ago and liked the silence. Finally, there was a space where he could think, where he could hear himself outside of the meaningless busywork. Here, Nick found he liked being alone more than anything else. This routine path allowed him the availability to mentally free himself from an unrelenting schedule, from the excessive everyday drama, from the life he didn't want for a few hours at a time, at least. Line after line, a comforting direction into the future, at least on the I-10, a solid direction was pointing where to go next.

Nick appreciated the quiet to think, to dream, to wonder what it could be like outside of this truck anyway, to imagine he was somewhere else. Surely, there were productive happy people out there who didn't crave the separation and the silence, who didn't wonder if they had trapped themselves in an obligation from which there was no escape. Ultimately, he just wanted to do the right thing. He had worked his whole life and desired to end up in a place where he was truly free. In these simple moments, hands on the wheel, external freedom seemed like something Nick had finally grasped.

Yet, strapped and buckled, physical restraints also reminded him of the bondage where he found himself trapped: alimony payments, visitation schedules, guilt and anger. Restraints that he would never let anyone see how much it bothered him belted into the driver's seat. Tied to the movement of his boss's vision, chained to a woman that would eventually take everything from him, trapped by a responsibility that he couldn't escape, whether he liked it or not—was this what he called freedom? Running his fingers over the faded American flag sticker proudly displayed on the dash—was this freedom when he didn't know even where he was ultimately going in life, on this road, in this job, with his nonexistent family, or why he should keep driving? But was he free to do any other thing?

Nick did choose some things: this job, for example, as opposed to another soul-sucking desk job. The trucking gig paid better, and he didn't have to play around with the corporate desk façade, this city instead of that one. It appeared like some of his choices were an intentional direction in life. He chose that crazy woman to marry when he was young and stupid. However, it was clear that he reaped the incredibly painful consequences of that decision. Nick was free, maybe, at least once upon a time, to make the choices for his path in this life.

The freeways were quickly dividing the road in front of him. He was supposed to go left down I-84 to get the delivery to the drop-off location by tomorrow morning, but he just didn't want to. Probably, now that he thought about it, the rebellion arose simply because it was something that he was expected to do. Not tonight. He wanted to go to the right. So what if the delivery was a day or two late? In a moment of resistance to the constraining cosmos, he could still direct his hands, this truck, and the next steps of his life. Satisfied for a moment, he was content with his decision down the freeway toward a tiny bit of freedom.

But was he free to choose whatever he wanted? There were the places Nick had been required to be, too many things he was not free to do. When he didn't feel like it, when he didn't see results or progress, the consequences of his decisions tethered him now to a life of monotony, frustration, and dullness.

It was getting dark. He took a swing of bitter, cold coffee. This road looked exactly like all the other nighttime roads he had been driving for the last seven years. Despite the attempt at caffeination, his vision glazed over. Nick didn't even realize the outside world had gone blurry. He clearly saw the future, the past, the starry night out the windshield, in the dark. He saw his young sons running toward him at the park when they were small. He saw his wife back when she was beautiful, before he couldn't stand her disapproving eyes. He saw his mother smiling. She held his chin and lightly kissed his head good night. He saw things and choices that he never had the opportunity to participate in. His childhood cul-de-sac, the color of his son's hair, the black, empty midnight dotted with far-off lights.

He saw many things in that split second of night. People and places and colors and feelings. They were all a part of who he was, a life received and not always intentionally chosen. He saw dark and light. He saw evil and good. He saw the other side of the highway, a surreal mirrored truck driving directly toward his own. Like a dream, more real than anything else, he watched as crumbling blue metal disintegrated into his front grill. He didn't choose this direction for his path, his destination. Sprinkling lights and numb colors suddenly overtook his senses—things that he had never seen or felt before. Smashing glass, slow motion. There was another man belted to the opposing truck. Nick could see his face. He could reach out of his cracking windshield and touch his terrified face. He met another nameless man, driving another meaningless truck in the middle of another meaningless night. And in their last breath, it was clear to both drivers that they were not completely free. Death had finally overcome their every lie of freedom.

*****

And we must ask, is anyone really free to choose anything when the whole road ahead crashes head-on into dreams, when, in a free world, one wouldn't have to deal with the consequences? But sometimes, it doesn't work like that because no one has been released from responsibility and consequence and uncontrollable chance. Roles, justice, inevitable roads are something more than what can be accomplished by simple choices.

And either way, for good or bad, your choices don't just affect you. There are people that will be helped or hurt. Children, spouse, friends, the web of relationships bind you to others. So there are limitations to what you can create as your reality. You will carry the weight of memory and ramification with you forever, and you just might have to say it out loud. You are not completely free to move about the world like you once thought.

But everyone wants to be free to choose; free to do this, not that; free to say this, not that; free to go here, not there; free to pursue the things that make one happy and live the best life. Let freedom ring equal opportunity for all. Life, liberty, and happiness, of course, without negative consequences—this is the freedom that is desired.

But looking around, there are flaws in this supposed freedom. You are not uninhibited to do whatever you want. You are not unrestrained to go anywhere you please. You are not encouraged to say anything that comes to mind. External restraints, internal limitations, imposed controls, self-inflected boundaries, time, place, and nature all have a hand in the restraints. Even if you know what will make you happy, you are not necessarily free to live that reality.

Certainly, there are options to make choices, but you do not exist in a vacuum. Bound by measures of good and bad, right and wrong, acceptable and unacceptable, the law of the land, of God, of nature, your freedom is constrained. Legislated freedoms are prescribed in detail, masking their ugly side of restrictions. Balanced transactional justification weighed by a righteous judge is the only way in which to keep freedom alive and fair in this country.

Furthermore, simple observation shows us that every single person on this planet has been born into a situation beyond their control. We know this; it is not shocking. Born into a privileged house with abundant opportunity, born in a third-world country, barely able to survive on the withering fruit of the dying land, cast upon a situation in life, whether determined by birth order, neglectful parents, disabling disease, or uninteresting monotony—there are some situations that have left us with little choice, if any.

But modern freedom is confusing and even lies to you, especially in a choice-centered culture. Freedom's blanket wraps everything from choosing a breakfast cereal to voting for president, to choosing which pronoun to use in your Instagram profile. Behind the disguise of freedom of choice is the situation in life that one discovers. Under the surface of unbound decisions, we must deal with the pieces of life over which there is no control. Can you choose to be or not to be? Are you free to choose to be whatever you desire? Are you really choosing for yourself?

Spinning the wheels, directing the vehicles to a place on another Monday morning, scraping part-time jobs together to make ends meet—are any of these the freedom that has been desired? But we continue to fight for our own freedom, especially in an age of modifying our body parts and choosing our genders, changing our story to reflect something that we feel, believing the lie that we can choose who we were made to be.

The challenge with confessing God's story is admitting that you exist in the midst of a reality where you do not have ultimate control. You have been created by another, bound by the vision and physical construction of another, born into this world, placed on a road, a much longer timeline than your own. Whether under the disguise of political freedom or captive in physical oppression, you are a slave. Not one is free, no matter which king or authority you serve. There is no system on this earth that will produce the freedom for which you hunger. Stubbornly, you will struggle to learn that you can't just choose anything that is to be desired.

> So God created mankind in his own image, in the image of God he created them; male and female he created them. God saw all that he had made, and it was very good. (Genesis 1:27, 31)

Mankind was created in the image of God. This was good; this was perfect. This was not their own free choice, not at all. It was a complete gift, fully given by the Almighty God. Life, breath, creation, love, dominion, water, trees, relationship—all of this was determined and decided for them at the beginning of time. They did not select the abundant life into which they were placed. But it happened to be the truest form of freedom any human since then would ever know. Because in the goodness and mercy of the Almighty God, His creations are free to be exactly what they were meant to be.

However, the man and woman in the Garden took the chance to believe the lie of freedom. The serpent tempted them to decide their own fate. The lies of the evil one sprouted desire in their own hearts. Let's be like God, knowing good and evil. Let's be like God, creating our own circumstance. Let's be like God, free from the deadly consequences spoken by the Almighty God. The great lie was spoken. And unfortunately for all of us, it was trusted.

> (The serpent) said to the woman, "Did God really say, 'You must not eat from any tree in the garden?'" The woman said to the serpent, "We

> may eat fruit from the trees in the garden, but God did say, 'You must not eat fruit from the tree that is in the middle of the garden, and you must not touch it, or you will die.'"
>
> "You will not certainly die," the serpent said to the woman. "For God knows that when you eat from it your eyes will be opened, and you will be like God, knowing good and evil."
>
> When the woman saw that the fruit of the tree was good for food and pleasing to the eye, and also desirable for gaining wisdom, she took some and ate it. She also gave some to her husband, who was with her, and he ate it. (Genesis 3:1–7)

The lie of freedom was that man and woman believed they could be something different, that they had some sort of control and design over their own life. The lie that the serpent encouraged was that they were wiser than the Almighty God. They had found a wisdom that released them from the gift of just being human.

But their supposed freedom didn't work. They couldn't choose to be anything they desired to be. Immediately after Adam and Eve assumed "freedom" in this cosmic story, they were painfully shown that they were never free. God spoke the consequences: pain in childbearing, strife between man and woman, hard work and sweat, and, yes, death for all—curses to be carried by them and all children born into this reality.

This is where imagined freedom as creatures is exposed. Man and woman were given this world and their blessings and their breath of life. Man and woman were, now from this point forward, trapped by deceptions of the enemy of God, the consequences of their disobedience, and a world that would continue to reflect the changed reality. There was no freedom as they understood it. God announced this changed world, a reality that cursed the man and woman and the ground they stood upon. But it wasn't just for this man and woman personally. It affected every generation that would be born after them. It entrapped every being that would ever breathe on this earth. Every creature now must battle this twisted reality. Every creature is bound by an external reality from which they cannot free themselves.

The whole world was changed as God spoke His words of judgment to His people, His words of disappointment, His words of the new cursed earth.

> I will put enmity between you and the woman, and between your offspring and her offspring; he shall bruise your head, and you shall bruise his heel. (Genesis 3:15)

The serpent's lie of freedom not only enacted a war on God's first people but also changed the existence of everyone involved. Proclaimed by God, this was the new reality, the new battle. The heavenly opponent, Satan, twisted the Word of God and deceived mankind. This one who has shown himself to be the enemy of God will continually fight with the children of man. Previously, the serpent was a beloved creation of the Almighty God under the loving rule of Adam. But God proclaimed that the animal and human kingdom would no longer be united and working toward the same goal. Now there is enmity between man, human, and beast. There is an angst. There is a disconnect that was not previously present. From now on, this enemy is bound to work woe on all of Eve's children. Since the beginning, he has enflamed the curses, encouraged doubt, spread lies, and dealt death to every offspring of woman.

Yet the serpent's lie has been the same from the beginning. You can be like God. You can be free from His words and His command. This temptation to take our choices for godlike decisions is hard to ignore. He has led you to also believe that you can have ultimate control over your own life and choices. Yet the realm in which you have control is embarrassingly small. In everyday life, you may have mistakenly chosen breakfast cereal and college preferences to be a bold declaration of universal self-sufficiency. Consequently, in the realm of the Almighty God, this leads to a misunderstanding in a relationship with Him.

Free will. Do you have the ability to believe in God or not? Can you make the decision to follow Jesus? Do you really have the will and discipline to take up your cross? You assume that you possess free will in all things, to choose heaven or hell?

There are certain options in our life, on our path, but we have never had unbound, unattached, self-sufficient freedom. In fact, the confusion of freedom is both a cause and consequence of the curse we struggle against. It is a misunderstanding that you can choose what happens with your life. Even in the world in which the first humans were created, this was never the case. There are choices but never in terms of whom you were created to be. There have always and only been two actors directing our epic story: God and what He has determined, Satan and what he has distorted. But even today, God's creatures still trip up on the false belief that they are the best-knowing gods of their own destiny. This is directly a consequence of the battle of the curse that all humans cannot escape on their own.

To believe that you are free is to place yourself as the highest authority—free above the rules you decide to submit to, free above the government you choose to listen to, free above the god you worship. Your illusion might work for a while. You can have certain freedoms in relation to the law of the land if you are not affected by the benefits and consequences of your actions. You can be free in relation to the bondage of others if you are not affected by their approval, their love, and their distrust. You are free in relation to your Creator if you are not subject to His words, blessings, or reality. But ultimately, you are not free. No living being is free from the One who created and sustains all life.

And yet this struggle is nothing new. In Holy Scripture, we often hear of feigned freedom that is really deep bondage to sin: struggles with the lie of freedom, the lie of Satan, and our darkened understanding under the curse. There are histories of people, societies, offspring of the woman that continually tell of this combat. It is the same story that has been told for ages and ages, over and over. And it certainly reflects our story, even today.

Centuries ago, St. Paul wrote a letter to the Romans, who were also fooled into believing the common tangled lies of freedom. They exchanged what was true from God with untrue and unnatural manifestations of reality. They began to worship dead and mute objects. They switched the definitions and functions of a naturally created man and woman. They took what was real and just denied it, telling untrue stories to themselves and to the world around them. They took it upon themselves to imagine they were free from creation, from each other, and from God. They believed that they could create their own world, own bodies, yet they were also trapped in a time and place that they could not escape.

> For although they knew God, they neither glorified him as God nor gave thanks to him, but their thinking became futile and their foolish hearts were darkened. Although they claimed to be wise, they became fools and exchanged the glory of the immortal God for images made to look like a mortal human being and birds and animals and reptiles.
> Therefore God gave them over in the sinful desires of their hearts to sexual impurity for the degrading of their bodies with one another. They exchanged the truth about God for a lie, and worshiped and served created things rather than the Creator—who is forever praised. Amen.
> Because of this, God gave them over to shameful lusts. Even their women exchanged natural sexual relations for unnatural ones. In the same way the men also abandoned natural relations with women and were inflamed with lust for one another. Men committed shameful acts with other men, and received in themselves the due penalty for their error.
> Furthermore, just as they did not think it worthwhile to retain the knowledge of God, so God gave them over to a depraved mind, so that they do what ought not to be done. They have

> become filled with every kind of wickedness, evil, greed and depravity. They are full of envy, murder, strife, deceit and malice. They are gossips, slanderers, God-haters, insolent, arrogant and boastful; they invent ways of doing evil; they disobey their parents; they have no understanding, no fidelity, no love, no mercy. Although they know God's righteous decree that those who do such things deserve death, they not only continue to do these very things but also approve of those who practice them. (Romans 1:21–32)

The Romans thought freedom was exchanging, renaming, exploring, as if they were free—sexual freedom, personal freedom, religious freedom, gender freedom, freedom of choice, freedom of speech, freedom from all authority. They traded the truth that was given to them, for a lie.

In response to their supposed freedom, God let them think they were free for a while. Their distorted view of freedom turned into His judgment that they received. The self-knowing people thought it was good but actually served them eternal separation and death. They became deaf to God's words of reality. And their own false-free fantasy led them far, far away from who they had been created to be.

The lie of freedom. Those who believe it are forced to follow the bondage of their own desires. Creatures are unable to break free from their sins of past, present, and future. And those who cannot recognize this lie remain trapped within themselves to find righteousness. Inside their own hearts and souls, they are emboldened in the tempting offerings of Satan. Chained to their own shadows, they have forgotten the ancient battle to hear God's Word. They ignorantly chase what looks like freedom, binding themselves to death.

Is this freedom true and real, believing that they could escape the confines of God's order, God's Law, His promise? Was it only imagined freedom? God left His people alone to do exactly what they wanted. He left them to create their own future. When He left them alone, there is nothing good about that. People who are free to recreate their existence will attempt to be their own god. He let them reimagine His creation. He let them take what He gave and changed it into something else. The gift that He gave, that He loved, that He knew was the best for his people. God let them corrupt it into something else.

But the more disturbing aspect of this desperate scramble of delusion is that the Almighty God just watched. He stood back. He let them. He let them destroy His whole world freely. And like every generation before, the people couldn't help but twist it into lies, sickness, and death. He let them. And here, the people were engrossed in the living lie that they had found twisted freedom from the protection of the Almighty God.

God's judgment is giving His creatures up to their own desires. They can't see anything else, focused on their own hungers and passions. The promises of the Almighty God fade into the background. The Word of God doesn't seem like it matters up against the sovereign desire of the self. When God allows you to do exactly as you feel in your own heart and head, that is the same point where God is letting go.

Even for you, the serpent's lie has been the same from the beginning. You can be like God. You can be free from His words and His command. After the deception of knowledge, this is exactly what we are bound to do, exchanging the wisdom of God for an unhinged knowledge of yourself, believing your own god-heart to tell you what is good and true, believing the lie of Satan that you are the authority. This battle of the serpent rages on, twisting the truth of God. So you misunderstand. The ancient Romans misunderstood. The generations before and after will continue to seek knowledge that is not wisdom.

> None is righteous, no not one.
> No one understands; no one seeks for God.
> All have turned aside; together they have become worthless; no one does good, not even one. (Romans 3:10–12)

No one is righteous, not even one, St. Paul continued to write the same sad story of unbelieving and ignoring, confusing freedoms and autonomy, good and bad, and personal choice. Of course, there are varying degrees of how evil we can be or have been. It's not completely equal how destructive to ourselves and others we can end up. Some of us have made better temporal choices than others. But no one is righteous, not even one. Before a Heavenly Father that judges every act, in public or in secret, you are not telling the truth if you say you have no fault. You are seeing clearly if you recognize that you have wrongly trusted in yourself.

No one is righteous. This is exactly what the great battle is all about. If the devil can encourage you to believe that you are a god, that you have found your own wisdom, that you can be free from the hand of God, then the devil has won. He will continue to tempt you to believe that you are righteous, that you are free, and that you can choose a better reality than the one God has given.

In fact, the areas of your life that you think you have done the best are the most dangerous places. Here you may get used to looking at the incomplete works you have done with your hands. You might begin to trust in your success as righteousness by which God must be impressed, inching toward godlike status to contend with the one true God. The stark reality is, even in your best works, you have fallen short in knowledge in thought, in word, and deed according to God's holy standards.

So in your striving and trying, you will not find freedom. In your leaving or hiding or ignoring, you will not find freedom. For a culture obsessed with the ideas of freedom, it doesn't import the knowledge of what means to be truly free.

The cosmic joke is that creation and the natural definitional order are inevitable in this world. Creatures are made by a Creator. God made the planet and trees and the animals and the people. You did not create yourselves. You are not able to entirely remake yourselves. You are just insanely bad at keeping God in charge of it all. And ultimately, you were and never will be free from your God-declared identity.

But even those who listen to the Word of the Lord always struggle to hear His wisdom. His people, from the very beginning of time, have been engaged in the struggle of desiring their own freedom. His people are not outside of the reach of the curse, even though they remember His creative hand, even though they try to listen to His Word. Confusion, pride, misunderstood freedom—these realities also plague the children of God.

Great heroes of our ancient faith have misunderstood their identity, paths, and God's promises. Long ago, God foretold faithful Abraham and his wife, Sarai, that they would have a child, that they would have an incredible number of children, more than the stars in the sky, more than the sands in the sea. And yet Sarai had no children for so long. They believed God's Word, sure, but it wasn't happening as they wanted. It wasn't happening at all, in fact.

Sarai couldn't have children. She stared into the dark every night, wondering what she could do to make this go better. She wanted a baby. She was sure this was part of God's plan. She needed to help along the promise. She needed to make a choice for the future, for her future, for the future of the promised seed for God.

> But she had an Egyptian slave named Hagar; so she said to Abram, "The Lord has kept me from having children. Go, sleep with my slave; perhaps I can build a family through her." Abram agreed to what Sarai said. So after Abram had been living in Canaan ten years, Sarai his wife took her Egyptian slave Hagar and gave her to her husband to be his wife. He slept with Hagar, and she conceived. When she knew she was pregnant, she began to despise her mistress. Then Sarai said to Abram, "You are responsible for the wrong I am suffering. I put my slave in your arms, and now that she knows she is pregnant, she despises me. May the Lord judge between you and me." (Genesis 16:1–5)

God let her try her own plans. He let her test this lie of freedom. He gave her up to the desires of her own heart and the solution of freedom. God promised children. She wanted children. This was not a complicated game. She must have needed to work it out in her own way.

And Sarai thought. She cried. She was mad. She was tired. She didn't want to do it like this, but it seemed like the only option. All the tools were suddenly laid at her fingertips.

It was better that Abraham had a child, a son, an heir. She reasoned that it was prideful and selfish to believe that she must be included in this plan, when God could make anything happen, whether she was there or not. She tried, Sarai did, to be a righteous mother and wife for the sake of the greater good. She thought she could lay aside her personal feelings to encourage her husband to produce the family that would be good for everyone. She thought she was free to do it by herself.

It was not a freedom she wanted but one she believed was necessary. Abraham would have a child. Abraham should sleep with her maidservant. Her husband must be joined to a more productive and blessed mother than she would ever be.

Sarai's heart fell deep into her throat that evening when the door closed without her. The quiet evening by herself, imagining what she felt like, thinking about how he touched her. Sarai tried not to envision the passion that had to be conjured between them joining together for the sake of their promised child.

But it was important for the future, for the promise. Her personal feelings should not overcome the greater purpose. She freely chose this. It seemed like the best option to get what they all wanted.

It worked. A baby was born. God allowed their supposed freedom to prevail. And Sarai was destroyed on the inside by her freedom manifest.

Because now it was clear that she wasn't the one that God would use. She wasn't the one that Abraham needed. She wasn't the one meant to be a blessed mother.

In her own freedom, her identity was lost. When she tried to find herself, she did the opposite. Mother of the promised, she was slayed by her own hand. By naming and creating herself, she wrecked it all. God gave her up to the desire of her heart. Now it just felt like jealous anger.

She was angry at her faithful friend, jealous of their success, impatient with the promise of God, sick of herself.

The story could end right here. Teaching this couple a horrifying lesson, God could have left Sarai alone and angry. He could have ended this great salvation story a million times over, generations ago. He could have left Adam and Eve hiding in the bushes. Just like He could have left Abraham with a child, which was not the promised one.

God did not leave Sarai alone forever. He did not allow her to remain in judgment of the freedom that she wanted for herself and her family. He did not leave her alone to simply teach her a lesson about her freedom. He kept His promise despite her reach for freedom. He still enacted His plan of mercy. To be sure, there was sorrow, pain, and regret in her choice. She didn't understand it all. But something remained, and it was not right. And she was caught in the consequences of bad choices but never too far from the hand of God.

Just as God did not leave the first man and woman alone in the Garden. Even after the first terrible aftertaste from the lie of freedom when man and woman first discovered they were not completely free, they were not alone. He would not leave His people alone in their misimagined freedom. They ran. They hid. He found them. And thankfully, they were never free.

Scared in the bushes, experiencing the new reality, responsible for the choice they had made, unable to run away because they were not free—they were not released. They were not the only ones in charge of their story and their reality. They were not able to choose where to go next. They couldn't choose what to be or not to be. But they now knew a new world, the stinking afterbirth of disobedient choices.

Freedom, escape, abandoning of responsibility—that doesn't change what you've been given to do. And running away from it doesn't excuse anyone from the responsibility and consequences of where you've been placed in the story. Even just admitting your failures doesn't wipe them from your record. Soon enough, you will realize that there is nothing to do. You can't free yourself.

But everyone becomes lost like this, at least for a moment, for a time, for a purpose. The lie of freedom makes you believe that you are doing exactly what you want to do and what is best for you. You imagine that it is possible to live free from the external accountability to Creator, to society, and to your neighbor. But unbound freedom only leaves you lost in yourself. To ignore it is to be untruthful. Freedom and independence are the oldest temptation into disobedience. And everyone falls for it: Sarai, Adam, Eve, you, me. But ironically, the solution to your destructive, misunderstood freedom is solved by the mercy of God.

Once you can understand the bondage in which you live, then you may begin to desire real freedom that only a powerful Savior can deliver. Freedom from failure, freedom from judgment, freedom from injustice, wrong made right, excused from certain death, reparations made with a silent and far-off God—this is the only freedom that actually matters. This is the freedom that will change your everyday. This is the freedom that makes all the difference.

Based on your own heart and experience, you will never enjoy a freedom like Christ's forgiveness. It is unblemished by your bad choices, your good deeds, your careful morality, your death-deserving sin. Freedom in Christ is the parallel universe that is bound by no chains at all, limitless, released, unrestricted. Freedom is a simple word, no rules, no requirements. Freedom then wholeheartedly despairs the hopeless situation where everyone finds themselves. Freedom recognizes the heavy chains that cannot be broken by the right law or person or situation or government or place or time. Freedom is found in the release from curse, sin, and death.

God sent a Savior that changed our reality, rewriting the story for every creation consigned to die. This act is a reversal of death itself. This Savior walks free from a prison, a tomb that bound him temporally, death, sin, and shame. This Savior told us that was His purpose: to die and rise again. And this Savior said that He did it all for you.

You are free.

This is a righteousness apart from the law of good and evil, apart from faithfully following God's plan, apart from being the godlike perfect one. The only freedom from God's rules and orders is death. Your will and actions fail because you are not the righteous one. Death is the only thing that releases you from the consequence of the curses, from the consequence of your sin. Death is true freedom. Death is the end of the judgment of God.

Christ died for you. Christ took your death and made it His, saving you from the consequence of sin, the consequence of guilt, the consequence of the curse. He died to stop the future of eternal death. Christ was risen to eternal life, and He promised you would follow Him. Now you are free from the headship of the devil. His lying words mean nothing now that Christ has spoken for you. You are free from the fear of judgment because Christ was judged victorious for you.

Christ is the one who gives you righteousness apart from the law of God. He is born into your reality. He died, and He rose again. Because of this, you will never have to die like that. Your righteousness will not satisfy God's rules. You do not have to possess the knowledge of God. He did not leave you alone to do that. He never has.

You are forgiven. And that is freedom from fear, sin, the devil, and death. Forgiveness frees you to be the creature you were originally made to be right now, today.

You are free from worrying if you have been good enough because you haven't, Christ has; free from checking off a list of requirements to be a good person because you aren't, Christ is; free from the depression of failure because that is not the end of the story, Christ is. You are free from believing that you must control your destiny.

True freedom is living with the assurance of your complete forgiveness in Christ. Autonomous freedom is the lie that leads to despair. Beyond our every border and counsel, past every accountability partner, more than any moral standard, there remains no ill consequence for you in Christ. Because of His death and resurrection, because of the Savior's victory for you right now, the new reality is freedom of life, liberty, and happiness until eternity.

Freedom means that you are not bound to your decisions, good or bad. Freedom means there is something greater promised to you No matter what you do, your life has been set right. Freedom, for you, is no longer synonymous with your personal choice. Rather freedom is a release from the cursed world, from our cursed relationships, from our cursed bondage to the devil, and from the curse of death. Here and now, your freedom is everlasting peace with God.

You are free.

And the terrible and sad reality is that you fail to remember where true freedom originates. You are burdened in a world that must substitute and provide for the lack of mother, father, friend, provider, or confidant. You fall again into the lies of freedom, and there is much that is given up without even knowing it. When God gives you up to your own desires, your future is uncertain, and your future is deadly. In your perceived freedom, you think that you have complete control. You do not. You never did. At the end of the day, you do more damage when you believe that you are free.

Truly, there was never autonomous freedom, not like anyone thought. It was always part of a bigger plan, a greater creation. You were never balancing on the fence of your choices. You are either overtaken by your desires, or you are overtaken by God. There is no in-between. God knows this. So does the evil one. And yet, as the enemy still leaves you bruised and bloody in this lifetime, the greater battle is already won.

There is nothing to fear when you consider the righteous rules of the Creator, when you hear the Word of the law of God that terrifies and frightens you. There is nothing to fear when you hurt one another and hurt yourself. In the freedom of Christ, there is no death for you. You can just be, enjoy and love.

You are free.

This is true freedom from the ultimate consequences of sin, the sin you can't avoid; from the epic battle with the devil, the serpent, the sin of the Garden, because it is over. You are totally free from death, even though your sinful actions still deserve it. You are free from paying the eternal consequence because Christ, the promised Son, has already made you righteous by His blood. You are free no matter how you fail. You are free without your permission or consent. He enacted your freedom in a way that absolves you from the irreversible bondage of the curses. You cannot reverse them. Your deeds will not reverse them. God has not reversed them, but the Son has made it right again for you.

You are free. And you are bound in the victory story of His freedom.

Children Are Painful

One night, my seventeen-year-old daughter looked me in the eyes and said, "Why have you ruined my life?"

Tears were streaming down her face, and she wouldn't say anything else. While this is not an uncommon story, especially if you have been a parent to a teenage girl, I didn't have the words to respond. I had given up school, jobs, dreams, prestige so that I could be at home with her as she grew. Maybe, just maybe, she ruined my life. Spoken in haste, we were both bruised and bloodied in our ever-so-common relationship struggle.

Our reality certainly includes pain in childbearing. Specifically, part of the curse God proclaimed to the woman in the Garden, all relationships with our children are absolutely less than they were originally created to be. But it is easy to distract ourselves with the temporary answers, new parenting philosophies, endless counseling sessions, or bribing their love with the newest technology. While not one of these things are evil or bad, this confirms that we all struggle with our children.

The answer is messy, but it is finished. Fighting, crushing, bruising, until victory—the son of God bleeds out for us to repair the relationship between mother, father, son, and daughter. Our gift of reconciliation reaches past the curses by the sacrifice of Jesus.

*****

Red swirling tails overtake the ripples of clear water. Ribbons of crimson twirl quietly in this silent moment—a secret flood, a hushed wave, a hidden current rolling smoothly beneath the surface. All by herself, Marie watches the scarlet dance, entranced by the simple beauty in the water, hypnotized by the simple horror of the blood.

She knows she should cry. It would be the right thing to do, but not just yet. The grief and pain will overtake her soon enough. No, for now she just has to watch. She won't let her eyes drift away from the blood and the water.

A sharp, unfamiliar memory stabs her in the gut as she watched another rosy curl unfold. She has been here before, watching, waiting, wondering. Suddenly, the cigarette smells and pounding music of the past colored her vision, remembering an earlier time. A younger, more confident, just as confused little girl sat here once before, spellbound by the red ripples; relieved, back then, to see the blood and the water.

Her mind and body were replaying the same terrible dream from the depths of her past. Numb in the moment, blank future ahead. Again blinded by the death that poured from her own body. She once thought that suffering could be solved by a little pill. And so, once upon a time, Marie took that pill seven weeks after an impulsive hook up, seven weeks after her first child was conceived.

She has been here before, peering deep into that tiny sea of water and blood. Remembering, impatiently watching, waiting, wondering. Remembering, being tired of studying every red swirl. Remembering, the vomiting, cramping, bleeding. Sick with herself for wanting to return to the unexamined life on the other side of her bathroom door. Searching desperately for that clot to freedom drowned in the water.

Tonight, the squeezing, crushing, throbbing, stabbing. When would this end? Little, tiny chunks of a "once upon a time" was expelled one at a time. The minutes seemed like eternity, dripping from her being until the finale. When she couldn't speak, she couldn't do anything but double over, Stretching, pushing, plunging, and splashing.

The baseball-sized mass didn't float. It was hard to even see really what it was amid the opaque blood liquid below.

But tonight, she now felt a pain deeper than just the excruciating contractions. It radiated from her side deep into her stomach, piercing her heart so much that it was hard to breathe. That huge fist of flesh in the ruddy water resembled someone that she tried to forget so many years ago. Marie was afraid to look too closely. Was that a little hand or her imagination? Entombed tonight by her own dead flesh, she remembered that a tiny unlived life lay stilled under the surface of this water.

"I wonder if anyone cares that someone died here tonight," she whispered in her mind, regret for her foolish choices, rage for her naive hopes in a beautiful future. Waves of uncontrollable sobs intermittently were hushed with a hypnotized silence—one moment of hopes and dreams, one moment of desperate anger. *Why did this happen?* She tortured herself, wondering. She wanted to love a baby. She wanted to be a mother. She wanted a stable relationship. She wanted a dog that met her with the morning coffee. She thought they were just the little things, the little normal pleasures that everyone else forgets they even have. *What's wrong with me?* she wondered all too often.

Her knees ached, frozen in one position on the ceramic tile floor, crouching on that brown fuzzy bathmat for too long. Licking the edge of her dry mouth, tasting bile-coated cheeks and teeth. But she couldn't move. She didn't have the strength. Well, she didn't have the will. Why should she get off the floor anyway?

Marie knew she had been wrong. She knew she had chosen poorly. She had a destructive past. She did not take care of her body. She didn't even pray anymore. Considering the blood, her life, and this death, she couldn't help but realize she had deserved this. In hindsight, she now knew there would certainly be consequences for her unmentionable sins.

Back and forth, her mind screamed and condemned and cried to a silent, distant God. Wrestling with both the hideous sins of her own hands and the dreadful circumstances inflicted upon her, she had no answers. She couldn't look down. She couldn't look away.

Did she dare to flush the toilet, wash the sin away? Or was she brave enough to properly embrace and properly bury the baby she almost had? The dark water in the cold, white bowl submerged her future, present, and her past. Marie was poured out, dried up, tired.

Too exhausted and sore, she lay down on the bathroom floor. It smelled like sticky sweet soap that reminded her of baby powder. She gagged and closed her eyes. And the bathroom horror scene disappeared behind her heavy eyelids for a moment.

It wasn't clear how long she had been out. Her head hurt. The light was left on and felt like it was stabbing her eyelids to open. She didn't want to open them. In her perfect world, a dream guy would have been there, scooping her off the cold, dirty floor, tucking her safely in a warm bed. In a merciful world, he would be stroking her hair and saying, "I'm right here. We can make it through anything together." He would have tears in his eyes, bearing this pain alongside her.

But tonight, she was alone—no husband, no boyfriend, no child, no one. She was sickened by the justice of an unfair reality, face-to-face with the great enemy: death. He had a hold of her womb. Death twisted her hopes and disappointed her dreams yet again. Her babies. Why did God have to take their unbreathed lives? Not even old enough to speak or act for themselves yet. What did they do to deserve such a punishment?

More sickening than that was her participation. Whether she wanted to or not, her will, her neglect, her avoidance, her good intentions, her very body had become a carriage of destruction for her unborn babies. Death was delivered by their mother, who was built to give them life.

At least Marie could conceive that she deserved it. It would be a rational response from the universe to her irresponsible history: the strange men, the questionable drugs, the procedures disguised as responsible prevention. Ignorance was no excuse for the consequences of today. It was a terrible and deep reminder of how very far she was from being the ideal woman, the ideal mother. Hindsight taught her much more than she could ever say out loud. But even now, after years of healing, her body was still broken, hurting, and lacking. In her faraway past, she willingly killed her child. And tonight, unwillingly, she watched another life drift away.

*****

Yet the problem is rooted deeper than the individual saga of a single reckless girl. This pain, this regret, this despair is not only for the mothers who have actively neglected their own children or even the children that had not yet come to be. It's not only a problem for those who can discern a moment of evil in their own hearts and hands that would point to such a punishment. The great sorrow of all is that people have both willed and inherited this suffering, the anguish of childbearing.

Women who have done everything right are barren and tormented. Women who are ill-equipped for the task are fruitful. Women who sacrifice for their offspring are despised and unrewarded. Women who try to live their own life are constantly stricken by the pain their children are able to cause.

Women and men, together, have been crafted to do something amazing. By their flesh and blood, they are the cause and vessel by which every new life is created. And it was supposed to be wonderful. It was supposed to be easy. It was supposed to be joyful and fulfilling.

> So God created man in his own image, in the image of God he created him; male and female He created them. And God blessed them. And said to them, Be fruitful and multiply and fill the earth and subdue it, and have dominion over the fish of the sea and over the birds of the heavens and over every living thing that moves on the earth. And God saw everything that he had made and behold it was very good." (Genesis 1:27–28, 31)

It was good that man and woman would be fruitful and would fill the earth, that a woman would have babies, and that new life would spring from her body. A man was formed directly for this task and completely complimented by a woman. Their bodies fit perfectly together for the ultimate act of union, joining in pleasure, in purpose, in the needful creation of new life and breath. Man and woman were certainly made in the image of God and given His unique ability to bring forth another creature. This was very good.

And it is still good even today. Creation of new human life happens in everyday life by physical flesh and blood and bodies melding together. Even today, there is rejoicing at the birth of new life. The generations continue to spin round and round, just as they were meant to do.

But at the same time, the struggle and lack cannot be hidden for long. The pain of children and childbearing comes to the surface in everyday experience, hearkening back to the prescription God announced in the Garden of Eden.

> To the woman (God) said,
> "I will surely multiply your pain in childbearing;
> in pain you shall bring forth children." (Genesis 3:16)

Sin-wrecked bodies now wrestle to live in this world in response to the new reality brought on by the curses. The hurt is real that we now only hear from the story in the Garden. A clear and present mark of the punishment for sin certainly includes pain in childbearing. The torment as another body rips and tears through her own to gasp for new life. The pain a woman may endure emotionally and expectantly when childbearing is not fruitful, and she is left lonely. The pain that her children will inflict on her years and years after they have left the inherent protection of her womb and arms. The pain of shameful regret and hatred when an unwanted blessing graces her womb. Childbearing hurts at every turn.

The mother who is not, and the mother who is—all women experience this pain to some degree. It is the pain of this rearranged fallen reality, no matter how we try to ignore it, no matter what medical advances we take to repair it, no matter how long we can put off realizing it. We were created in the image of God, yet now we embody that reflection as a failure.

Even more unfair is that this inheritance of pain is not always directly related to actions, good or bad. A woman can be wonderful and will still reap pain. She can choose badly and will likewise bear the scars of this punishment. God's judgment upon His creatures and His creation changed the whole universe. The way in which people and earth and animals connected was severed. The way in which God and humans would communicate was redesigned, not for the better. Suffering and regret infected the good and perfect relationships.

Adam and Eve probably didn't see it all right away. They directly disobeyed their Creator and walked out of the land of present and abundant gifts. It was strange, those first few weeks—working, sweating, fighting, frustrations. But it might have taken a few years, hardship upon hardship, to realize the depths of their depravity. Eventually, outside in the wilderness, Eve had a baby, a blessing and a struggle with the curse. And this was the same struggle that would be part of your own.

Little did this woman know, her pain in childbearing has just begun. Two baby boys were given to her, Cain and Abel. Each grew up so very differently, not always making her proud as a mother. The boys competed for the love of their parents and the love of God. How many times did her boys disregard her warnings? How many times did they choose the wrong path before her very eyes? How many times did Eve know she had messed up in their upbringing? Looking into their frustrated eyes, nothing she could do would take that away. There she stood, watching suffering and strife blossom in her own young family.

The sun was bright, but the day suddenly felt empty. It was nothing out of the ordinary, but the feeling was one that she could not put her finger on. There was an uneasy, sick feeling that she had grown to despise. It was quiet. And it usually wasn't quiet with the two growing boys engaged in work and play. It usually wasn't ever quiet.

She had seen the anger, earlier that morning, between her own two sons. Face-off tensions between brothers were not in short supply. When they were only a little smaller, it was wrestling and meaningless arguments. But the older they grew, Eve became more concerned. This was not quite right. Their desires were a little off. Their future was not secure. Their relationship with each other was broken.

Eve felt special and unique guilt for her children. She personally had failed them as a mother. She hadn't cared enough for them or encouraged enough patience for each other. Adam was seemingly not effective as their father. He hadn't taught them the right attitude or instilled the responsibilities of becoming a man. And both parents expected so much of their first little boys, the first sons of man.

> He shall bruise your head, and you shall bruise his heel. (Genesis 3:15)

The foretold promise from God echoed in the middle of the cursed reality. Man and woman repeated this promise to each other and to the generations that would come after. An offspring would crush the head of the serpent that deceived them. God promised.

Adam and Eve must have believed that one of their boys was the promised one. Both assumed that God gave a child who was the immediate answer, the solution. He may be the one who would crush the head of that lying serpent, the one who would finish the reign of evil, which lead this family into painful exile. So the struggle was worth it if this offspring could restore the good, unblemished world that Adam and Eve lost. It was worth it if one of her sons was the one to restore the primary beauty of God's creation. It was worth it if one of these painful children was the answer to all of their disappointed prayers.

Proud as Eve was, discouraged as she was, finally there came a day when her beloved sons went too far. Jealousy overcame this freshly turbulent household. One quiet day, Eve couldn't find her grown-up baby boy—the sweet little child she had remembered teaching to walk, to talk, helping him to make his first sacrifices to the great, Almighty God. She couldn't find him. Deep sickness hollowed her out, looking for her Abel.

His older brother, Cain, shuffled home with a distorted face. Her anguish grew when she saw the shell of the son who used to call her mommy—limping, bloody. What was this ache? Why did these blessings from God pierce her soul? Her children, she suddenly had to admit to herself, were not right. And it couldn't have been their fault alone. This pain, this failure, had to also be a reflection on her as their mother.

Overwhelmed, she discovered their deadly exchange. She couldn't help but take some of the blame. If she had been there, if she had said the right things after Cain's sacrifice was overlooked, if she had raised them a little better, then one of her dear sons wouldn't lie dead, then her only living son wouldn't be running away for his life.

Eve lost both of her children that day—the boys she poured her whole life into, focusing for years on caring for them. She had failed, and she couldn't solve the problems that her children were burdened with. She was still guilty that they were still guilty. She didn't solve anything. And her boys were gone.

As many kinds of pain there are for a mother, a father, a man, or a woman, it is certainly a problem that cannot be solved by you because it is knitted into the fibers of this fallen creation. Women will feel pain in regard to their children or lack thereof. It is inescapable. That in some way every creature will remember, that we have the mark of death and suffering, and the curses that we think we can escape will remind all of this terrifying truth.

If even the first mother could question her vocation, her calling, how much more do you question? So far away from the beginning, so much later after the introduction to sin. If even the first mother could consider that she was not effective for her children, then who are you to make out any better?

Ending up unworthy, unsuccessful. Not because you ever wanted to be. But it happens. You are unable to prevent it. That is a realization that all of us must face at one point in our lives. Failure—for things you have done and for things you have not done, both in your control and outside of your control. Failure will hold you accountable as a creature who has fallen short of the glory of God.

There is an abundance of books that will tell you how to do this all better. Be a better person. Be a better mother—more engaged, more beneficial, more Christian. Solve the complications found in this world. Unfortunately, that's not going to solve the greater problem once and for all. Definitely, you are free to try anyway. But eventually, despair will catch up with you because it didn't work.

Parenting books, proverbs, coffee cup quotes, and exhausted friends will only take this so far. Simply exposing the inherent problems can only destroy you to the point where you will have to seek a real solution. Eventually, you need more than a quick fix.

Who are you in this cursed world? Who are you, bearing the burden of paradise lost? Unworthy, missing the mark in practice and uncultured reality. You have failed, and that is essential to the understanding of where hope and comfort lie. It is an alternate reality, where bad and good have been neutralized. It doesn't seem fair. Some have tried so hard, sacrificed so much. Some have not. And in the end, it is all the same.

Carrying the curse, there is pain in childbearing. The power of pride, mothers become ashamed to share who they really are. But it's not beneficial to hide it, believing what God has said and what this life has proven to be. One must admit, humans do not act like the flawless creatures that God created.

But the answer lies outside of Eve, outside of her actions, outside of your choices, outside of your very own body and soul, outside of good advice and success stories. The solution to striving and disappointments are dependent on something entirely other than you. Validation and meaning end up being something entirely other. Exposed as a failure has served as a well-trod path by which all have been prepared for the truth.

All fall short, and the Lord of all makes it right. From the beginning, the story of a Savior is the external reality that redeems you and every curse that plagues the earth, including childbearing.

> Yet she will be saved through childbearing—if they continue in faith and love and holiness, with self-control. (1 Timothy 2:15)

This is how woman is saved, not by doing the act of having children. Childbearing is certainly laced with pain and disappointment. But the promise was also given to all mankind, every single woman in the Garden, that a child will crush the head, stomp on the plans of the evil one, that a Savior of creation will set things right again outside of her hands, despite her actions. This is the reason that a woman can still proudly hold her head high as a mother failed, because the actions of another will be the ones that save her. Childbearing, down the bloodline, birthing this particular son of God, is what will make all the difference.

But just by perfectly fulfilling her God-given role, that is not the means by which a woman will be saved. Following the law of God is not what will redeem her. Every list of "to do," she will be shown lacking every time. She can stay home with the children, cook all the meals, submit fully to her husband, and practice the perfect and right path. She will care for and honor her children and husband, allowing a great and merciful God to provide for her family through her own hands. It's a beautiful path, but it is not enough.

And even the most perfect and careful creature will fall to her hands and knees, that she has still not done enough, that her efforts do not produce the intended effects of faithfulness and reciprocal love, that her sacrifice, although the best she could have given, is still not enough to atone for the things that run out of control. It is not the answer to save herself, even by childbearing. This is not how God's mercy works.

At the same time, it is absolutely critical to understand that every person is entirely responsible for the sins she has done with her own hands. Just because failure and struggle are certain, she is the one to blame, even as futile as it seems. She will fail and sin no matter what. And even the perpetual brokenness that has been passed down from an ancient mother, Eve, should be paid for with the blood of today's ignorant mothers.

Suffering through childbearing is not the act that wins any merit for a woman. Suffering through childbearing highlights an inconsolable need that she cannot work hard enough to obtain. Pain in childbearing hints at the lingering promise of a Savior that her childbearing will be set right again in the future. There is a world to come without pain, without suffering, without tears, without bruises and blood.

After taking the forbidden fruit in the Garden, God was angry. He was sad. He was regretful. Father and mother had shared an unholy meal, excluding God, spurning His good word and His good laws. They ignored and disobeyed their Creator. They became a legion of gods unto themselves, declaring war by choosing their path forward. By this, God's children earned death for themselves and their families.

Yet God wasn't finished creating Adam and Eve. Consequences, sadness, and suffering, they made for themselves. But God hadn't stopped giving. For woman, He told her to look at the very thing that would hurt her the most: childbearing. The blessed new life from her body would rip, break, and burden her conscience, sting her with regret until death took them. Yet her hope for redemption would have to rest in childbearing. In the trials, she would surely endure because of her curse.

After their great sin in the Garden, Adam took the hand of the woman and gave her a new name. Her name reminded them both of this salutary paradox. Her body of death, who chose and betrayed the Creator of all things, will be the very body that brings forth life—the first life, all life, the life that would be eternal life. Her new name, Eve, meant mother of all the living. And truly, she would be.

There would be many more mothers since Eve would still be blessed with the struggle of babies, yet they would one by one bring more evil woes upon the world. New generations and fresh breath would utter lies, hate their parents, and continually curse God so much that God would come to repent of the lives He had made. But God keeps His promises, and He himself became flesh and blood to change this reality.

Once upon a curse, God entered into the womb of a mother—a mother who was not supposed to be one, at least not yet. This mother was only engaged to a man. She was not in the respectable position to have a baby at all. But here she was, illegitimately pregnant, acting the part of a prostitute. Everyone talked. Everyone knew.

This mother story was not starting off very well. Even her soon-to-be husband, Joseph, didn't know what to do with such a disgraceful woman, betrayed and shocked by the child that wasn't his. Pain and suffering in the birthing of the bastard son. Of God.

She didn't know what it was, but something felt funny inside, outside. The pain of childbearing had gripped this young girl outside of consent and outside of her time. The altered world wouldn't leave her alone. It hurt when her friends whispered, when her beloved man now looked at her with guilt and shame, when her belly stretched and her stomach ached. What had she done to deserve this? But then again, why did she think she would be an exception for any woman who had to endure the pain?

Mary was a sinful woman and a daughter of Eve. Childbearing and dealing with the consequences—for the birth of our Lord, it could have been so much cleaner. Mary could have been the good and perfect vessel, bearing the good and perfect Son of God. But rather, a bastard child grew in the broken body of Mary. This mother was slowly dying as an ashamed little girl, so that no one, not even the humiliated mother of God, could boast in herself. Paradoxically, she was saved through this particular childbearing. This is the ultimate birth of life for which Eve, mother of all the living, was named.

From the womb of Eve to the uterus of Mary, women are saved through childbearing. It had to happen in a practical sense that generations would be born, offspring of the first woman, sinful birth upon sinful birth, until the promised child would be born, the one spoken about by God in the Garden of Eden. This offspring would finally crush the head of the serpent and defeat death itself.

> He shall bruise your head, and you shall bruise his heel. (Genesis 3:15)

We are called to focus upon this childbearing. This son who was born of Mary and of God became flesh to free your flesh. He was a sacrifice to God, unlike any good person could ever offer. He was a payment for collective sins committed, for a cosmic separation that you could not escape and beyond the ups and downs of your own childbearing. He was a death to pain and suffering, in total, replaced with eternal life. This is the ultimate fruit of Eve's childbearing, a Savior, that whoever believes in him will not perish but have eternal life.

But the pain persists even today. Kids hurt mothers. Parents are messed up. It doesn't feel right, not yet. You will fight, as Adam and Eve did, as Joseph and Mary did, as your grandparents did. But there is more than just the injuries left from today. There is more than this present pain. There is a new life and a beautiful world to come. Jesus conquered death to dominate the forces that bruise your body. He rose from the dead and restored your story of eternal life. His blood, spilled on the cross, has set an end to these painful curses.

So, to overcome the curse, you must look right at it. Watch for the blood, the very substance that recalls death, your death, your children's death, your sadness, your kid's failures, everything that is wrong with our life. God points you to watch for the blood, the sacrifice, on the cross, the last death that Christ died for you.

Remember it dripping down the sweet temple of the Heavenly Father's baby Boy. Stuck with knife and thorns, snot and tears, pain that a mother could not wipe away. Slashed in the side by the men and women who were supposed to love Him. Suffocating and choking by the weight of all the hidden, unrecognized, ignorant and willing evil. Remember that blood. See His blood. Look right at it.

In fact, don't just watch it, says the ever-creating Creator. Drink it. Take that which flows out of His heart and soul. He has put it into yours. Christ's body and blood is given for you. Proclaim your undeserved life everlasting until He returns. Your life, your blood, and your sacrifice are not enough. Jesus says to drink His blood, drink His life. By the death and resurrection of Jesus, you have eternal life that is beyond this world of curses. You share His new life right now, reborn and renewed.

Those who believe in the Savior, outside of themselves, still struggle together in this time, on this earth. But they also live in paradise at the same time. Admit the depths of your sin, separation in our relationships, and know it has been made right only by Jesus. The sadness will only last for a night. Today you live with the taste of eternal consequences, life forever, not dependent on these daily circumstances. With an aching awe, remember your hope; remember His blood. It changed everything. Taste true freedom and true love, even while living in the middle the curse.

What Is Love?

All good stories explore this essential question. Love and the pursuit of it wraps around every striving, heartache, and victory that we experience in our relationships with other people. But every love relationship between man and woman, friend and family, has been tainted by curses in a less-than-perfect creation. Love, now, is misunderstood and destroyed between people that should enjoy an easy, natural connection. Sin, sinners, a sinful world stir our emotions and jealousies with each other. What is love if you cannot count on absolute trust? What is love if it must last beyond your feelings? What is love in a broken world such as this one?

The relationships we should enjoy with each other have been twisted, as proclaimed by the Creator in the Garden. After man and woman broke His heart in disobedience, God said to her, "Your desire will be for your husband, and he shall rule over you." This is not how love was made to work. Since then, we also misunderstand what love was created to be—that is, until we abandon our personal love patterns and listen for the One who first and always loves us.

*****

Sometimes she lost her mind, rinsing, chopping, gathering, stirring. What did all of it mean? She was feeling emotions that made her sick with every cut, slice, chop. Her knife pierced the soft flesh of a zucchini, marring the vibrant green skin to show its unimpressive white insides. Vegetable triangles scattered in the wake of her unconscious rhythm. Chop, chop, chop. Tiny mountains of colors and shapes created a landscape between her fingers. Natural destruction of the natural. But when she moved the cut onions from board to bowl back to board for the second time, it revealed that she was floating in thought beyond the moment.

It happened sometimes when Terra was cooking. Or maybe it happened sometimes when she was thinking. Her hands were busy, productive, doing the right thing, serving, chopping. But her mind was far away, wondering, imagining, angry, destroying, chopping. She didn't speak of the thoughts that crushed her. She didn't want to stay the course set before her. And so there was little connection between her two universes, except it was the same person they both plagued.

She had made this recipe for her family hundreds of times. There was no need to look at measurements or be too picky about particular ingredients. Failing tremendously in the beginning to make a proper pie crust was a necessary part of how easy it had become today. Thinking way back, she remembered carefully studying each teaspoon of ice water as it dripped into that dusty bowl of flour, not too sticky, not too dry. She pressed the film of pastry into the dish ever so carefully, weighing and measuring each carrot and onion and directing everything in just the right place. Intense focus and attention to detail were a thing of the past. Now it was an automatic ritual, vegetable pie made for those who didn't really even enjoy this one.

But considering the evolution of her dinner preparations, that's not where her mind had disappeared tonight. Him. He frustrated her deeply. At this point in her life, she thought it would have been better, easier, clearer. But her reflections tonight felt just as raw as a silly teenager. There must have been progress, wisdom, maturity in this quest for love after so long. How can it still feel so unsure and unknown after so many years? Hurt and jealousy—who is to blame? Where was the well-deserved rest Terra had expected in this stupid game of love, hunger, and affection? Why has this not turned out more satisfying?

There were a million reasons for her to be angry, accusations that she would most probably be justified to make. But she knew she shouldn't. In the end, she told herself, that wouldn't hurt any less. She watched the heartbreaking divorces of her dear friends. She heard the lonely cries of her victimized single sister. She had watched her parents swallow incredible insults for the sake of staying unhappily married. Laughing silently, she had never before allowed herself to think she would be like any of them.

What then? What was this love she expected?—someone to kiss her sweetly, someone to fight for her, someone to fix the car, someone hungry enough to eat this vegetable pie, someone to inspire her, someone to teach her things she couldn't imagine on her own, someone who wouldn't leave her alone in the dark, someone who wouldn't leave her alone in her thoughts, someone to reveal herself, unashamed.

And he was some of it, some of what she could understand love to be, parts, slices of what she needed, pieces of what she wanted. And maybe she was only some of it for him as well.

But what about the rest? When he wasn't really there. When he wasn't really hers. When hurt and pain crept back up to the surface. When her suspicions were secretly confirmed. When an unspoken reality stared them both in the face. When was enough ever enough? When are the pieces not enough? When does a chopped-up love become too much to bear?

Warm butter and onions sizzle beneath her tears. There are two ways to go about it: Speak or keep quiet, go or stay, get or give. But in the end, both will hurt. There is not one better choice than the other to avoid pain. There is not one path or person that will ever put all the pieces together. She has seen it too many times: how sad we all are, how lonely we all live.

But they say, love never ends. Whatever is this love that she now believes has ended? Patient and kind—was it never love to begin with? Not envious or rude—did love abandon her, or did she abandon love? Not irritable or resentful—she fears tonight that she may never be completely loved by another, just as she is.

Several pies made from then to now, across the many years, she absolutely lost her mind, right here, again. Tonight, she couldn't suffocate the sobs. Recalling many a silent night of chopping—scared of the hurt, terrified of enduring pain, afraid of the love that she may not have found. The love that she may never find.

There were too many rumors of what was. There were too many thoughts of what could be. She couldn't get out of her own head, couldn't get away from her own heart, away from the things that she imagined would make her happy. But tonight, she could only think how very hungry she had become starving for this thing called love. Could she ever taste something like it, even though it was supposed to be what she had been chewing upon for all these years?

What was love? Did she have it even though it felt incomplete and in pieces? Did she have love? Did she even want love, if this is what it was? What was love?

But whatever this was, it didn't quite work. That was clearer than ever. And she couldn't quite grasp it. She didn't know how to solve the problems. Her life was screwed up. And she couldn't do enough to make it into a better world, not for herself, not for the man she thought she once dreamed of, not even for her own family. Terra was so disappointed because love didn't conquer all, because she didn't know if she could possibly love anyone anymore, or if she ever really did.

*****

Everyone, to some degree, wants to be loved. You want to be in the forefront of someone's mind and to be the receiver of kind actions. But is this love, or is it a magical, unattainable thing that only a few can be lucky enough to experience in the right place at the right time, with the right person, in the right situation? Is this love?

Everyone endures the millions of emotions tied to this little four-letter word: sweethearts, parents, spouses, children, and friends. These are the people who supposedly love you and people that you, in turn, are supposed to love. And what does it mean when love doesn't seem to work out at all? Just as the curses cloud our real freedoms, the curses also confuse our desires for true love.

Knowledge says that true, eternal love cannot exist. There are too many obstacles. There are too many experiences. There are too many feelings, backgrounds, and people. Ultimately, their death will certainly end lives and love. Whole industries of relationship advice revolve around this struggle. Entire worlds of divorce lawyers and porn stars count on this curse to wreck lives. The devil plays games of shadowed love with idols of every shape and size, yet there remains a desire, an innate drive to find, to experience, to capture love.

From the beginning, man and woman, every human was created to love, first formed to love their Creator, following that they would love one another, a one-flesh union, person to person. When Adam saw his love for the first time, he proclaimed, "Bone of my bone, flesh of my flesh!" He realized, *She is me, and I am her. We complete each other.* The desire for oneness and closeness is derived from how man and woman were designed to relate to one another.

All of God's creatures were created for an unashamed, uncomplicated love. Man was head of creation; woman was formed to help. Together, they were the royalty over everything, Together, they complimented each other perfectly. Together, they were one flesh, unconsciously loving each other, unknowingly fulfilling the law of love with which God had blessed His humans.

As with every other good thing that God gave freely to His beloved people, the giving and receiving of love has also been pierced by the cursed destruction of sin. There was much to lose in love. Much was lost when man and woman forgot their love for God. Much that was beautiful changed into an insatiable hunger. In consequence of disobeying the gifts of the Garden, God declared the new reality for both man and woman in His words spoken on that fateful day. There was now an unbalance in love, a reflection of the selfish nature of all of mankind. Spoken to the woman, God reveled the complications of every relationship touched by sin.

> Your desire will be for your husband, and he shall rule over you. (Genesis 3:16)

A once easy, unquestionable relationship of love, trust, and understanding redefined reality by the taking and eating of the forbidden fruit. Severed connections now stood between God and His people, but specifically now between man and woman. Desire and power, strife and submission, the simple true love that was imprinted in the hearts of human kind was twisted up. The desire for power and the reaction of slavery and headship permeates marriages, children and kids, friendships, work relationships. The beautiful love that we all are designed to want is held captive in a groaning age of disappointment and emptiness.

Since then, every woman, the man, the child all wandered in a wilderness beyond the walls of the Garden, obsessed with receiving true love. She, he, you, and I have been built to expect a story of salvation where love is freely given, gladly received. We were created to long for an unconditional love that is pure. But in experience, in every relationship on this earth, love acts unequally, cursed in love, selfishly and savagely taking what each of us needs to survive.

This curse reminds sinners that this world has been changed into an ocean of turbulent self-centered emotion for all. Now we fight misguided desire, incomplete and conditional loves that only distract. We are eternally hungry even after eating the fruit that could never satisfy. Most of the time, it is too deep to ever see in ourselves or in each other. Our love is now selfish. It was not just the challenge of man and woman in the story of Genesis, but our sin flows into every broken relationship on this earth.

> Your desire will be for your husband, and he
> shall rule over you. (Genesis 3:16)

It is in a vague manner for God to curse His people and their relationships. There are many explanations about how this disjointed relationship actually takes shape in our world today. Some explain that woman will desire her man sexually and yet never quite have what she wants. Or perhaps she will desire roles contrary to men, seeking to usurp his power and do whatever she wants. It could be that a woman will hunger for the "bad boy" who desires to control her and pass over the "good guy" who will care for her. The curse may hint that men will continually always end up with control, and women will hate it. But whichever version of strife you have experienced in the struggle of relationship, there is a common theme of unsolvable dissatisfaction.

In more recent times, our struggle for love has extended beyond genders. No longer is it sufficient to talk about love only existing between a man and a woman. Same sex couples also desire a connection with another person, bone of bone, flesh of flesh. Political and personal campaigns in support of love now flood our world, and yet these efforts are also met with struggle, disappointment, and pain.

Our broken bodies continue to find new ways to solve this ache, to no avail. Hurting for love and acceptance, we now have the technology to take our problems into our own creative hands, changing our own body parts, genders, hormones. While these struggles with gender and sexuality stem from a variety of individual reasons, one thing remains: We all want to be loved. We want to love. We want to feel at peace in our own flesh and bones and bodies. We want others to love and accept, unconditionally, the person we are. But love doesn't always work, and we are all left brokenhearted.

Every generation has inherited the fallout of what we believe love should be. Our expectations do not meet up to what we experience inside ourselves or outside in the world. Every man, woman, and child relate in some capacity in this way. It is easy. It is all too natural to want to be loved. But it is not natural nor easy to actually love. As with our previous understandings, perhaps it is our fault, under the veil of the curses, that we have misunderstood what true love actually is.

The Word of God has a particular definition of love. The love ordained by the Almighty is not defined as a feeling or emotion but rather action.

> Love is patient and kind; love does not envy or boast; it is not arrogant or rude. It does not insist on its own way; it is not irritable or resentful; it does not rejoice at wrongdoing, but rejoices

> with the truth. Love bears all things, believes all things, hopes all things, endures all things. (1 Corinthians 13:4–7)

The movement of love is found in the verbs: acting, doing. According to God, love does not sit around, waiting to receive, but love is the actor. This Bible passage is not a description of love, as one looks to check off a list. Rather, love is acting patient, acting kind, not acting arrogantly or irritable or resentful. Love is performing patience. Love is showing kindness. It is active. It is moving.

This may run contrary to the things that we want to feel inside that we want to simply receive. We want these words to describe the love that other people give to us. We want patience and kindness to be the description of the love we appreciate. However, if love is defined by action, then it does not matter if it is felt. In fact, the act of love may be contrary to one's feelings.

A description of a love that is "patient, kind, not envious or rude" highlights the contrast to the many broken, grating relationships we are a part of. We wait for the feeling of patience and endurance. But what if it never arrives? We desire to be caught up in the emotions of hope and rejoicing, but sometimes we become weary when the path still looks dim. What is love? The feeling changes by the day, but the action of love is clear.

This is the curse and blessing of love: feelings do not define real love. And much to our frustration, love is not necessarily returned. Love is enacted by the one who gives and not always appreciated by the one who receives. Unemotional love doesn't mean it is inactive if it is not recognized or returned. Love isn't always reciprocal. And an unreciprocated love can be absolutely complete.

Furthermore, many of our relationships are absent of this kind of love. Love is an action for one another, with or without emotional benefits. When we focus on our self-centered obsessions for comfort and peace, then we have misunderstood the love that we were made for. Fear inspired by the curse leads us to protect our hearts in our relationships, dealing with our unfulfilled desires and angst, control, submission, and pain.

But all hope is not lost. We know it by ancient stories of sacrifice and acts of honorable love. These stories awaken a universal truth that humans are all meant to participate in. But what is treasured in these great love stories? What is the deep connection we recognize when true love wins?

She was a certain kind of beautiful, no doubt. Hosea could see why a man would want her, but it was definitely not what he found attractive in a woman. She was a little too rough around the edges. Her mouth parted with a too-seductive smile. Her black hair frizzed a bit on the edges, exposing the friction it had been accustomed to. And her eyes were glassed over, dull even when she smiled, as if they had grown stale. Hosea longed for fresh, clear eyes. Yet hers evoked sadness.

She was known, and they knew her with a condescending glance. She was named, but they were ashamed if they had to say it. Hosea knew what they saw, and so he was surprised when her name was spoken by the Almighty God into Hosea's life.

He was a helpful steward of the faithful—a prophet who was studied, learned, quiet, and calm. He heard the Word of the Lord. He listened to it. He believed it. He spoke it even when it was unpopular to be the one who feared Almighty God. He saw this as his mission and purpose, more important than anything else, to hear and obey the Word of the Lord.

And still, the Word of the Lord came to him. And he was incredibly confused.

> "Go, take to yourself a wife of whoredom,"
> said the Lord. (Hosea 1:1-2)

A prostitute—that was his reward? That was his inheritance for speaking the Words of his Lord? A woman who had been taken by so many other men that all knew him, and they knew her. This was his honor? He commanded love for a woman, a woman that probably would not be able to love him purely, innocently, the very way in which he desired from the bottom of his heart.

Her name was Gomer, the prostitute that Hosea was given to love. But it was not in any way that he wanted to love, mind you. Even though he was a prophet of God, he had dreams and desires. He had other women he would have been able to give the world to. But this prostitute, she was his gift from God to show love and experience love made for His man and woman.

They married. They connected. There were children, and they were a family. Baby after baby, God named their children, their hardships of love, in Hosea's call. "No Mercy," God named her. "Not My People," He called another. Suffering, story after story, the curse of soiled love bled from unfaithful mother to cursed children. Generation to generation, the challenge of love stained every relationship that this man of God touched.

And this is the story of Hosea with his streetwalker bride. Acting patient and kind, not envious or rude, showing love to one that should be undeserving of love, possibly devoid of all emotion. This is the love in which God cradles His whole world—His whole unfaithful, unloving, undeserving world. It is His action, and we just receive His love. It is His sacrifice, so that we will ever be connected to Him. God will be the main actor of our greatest love story.

That is true love.

Because the love story of Hosea is really the love story of God and His people. *"The LORD said to Hosea, "Go, take to yourself a wife of whoredom and have children of whoredom, for the land commits great whoredom by forsaking the LORD."* The love that Hosea was asked to give to his prostitute wife was a forgiving and cleansing love. This was the same unbalanced love that God has patiently shown His wayward bride, the people of Israel. He turns unfaithful hearts back to Him. He sacrifices Himself for the sake of His bride. Action, sacrifice, patience, kindness, bearing all things—that is true love.

The ultimate act of love is sacrifice. This ultimate story of love has been told. God loved the world so much that He gave His only Son. He knew, in this action, that His love would not be returned. God looked at His ungrateful creatures. And He loved patiently, kindly, bearing all things. Undeserving people, for whom love did not change who they were, these were the people for whom He showed love.

God gives up the flesh of His own Son. He enacted His love for those who least deserved it, for the sinners and those who have taken other gods as their own, for those who have prostituted themselves to idols other than the Lord of heaven and earth.

> For God so loved the world, that he gave his
> only Son, that whoever believes in him should
> not perish but have eternal life. (John 3:16)

Love, according to the Creator, is sacrifice, giving oneself for another. For God so loved the world... so what? Was He feeling happy with His creation? Feeling affection and pride for His people? Quite the opposite. What about the many times that God was grieved by the creation of His hands? What about the extreme times when God destroyed His creation because He was sad that He made it all in the first place? And yet we hear, God so loved the world with a sacrifice. He sacrificed His one and only Son.

Active love, as designed in God's creation of all people, is a desire rooted deep, whether you wanted it or not. The Lord of all acts with precision when He loves His creatures. It is not an emotion. It is not a neat, little dream. Rather, He loves with His own flesh and blood. He loves an undeserving prostitute, the undeserving nation of Israel. He absolutely knows His love will not be returned.

This is true love, sacrificing self for another, the action of love, kindness, patience, not envious or rude, bearing all things, knowing that he was taking a wayward lover who couldn't love Him the same way back. This is the enduring love of God, giving life to cursed sons and daughters who betray Him. That is love, committing to a wandering nation, a wandering prostitute, a wandering people who has been unfaithful. That is love, renaming a wretched woman who took and ate and shared the forbidden fruit. That is love, forgiving a woman who instituted the terrible drama of sin and death by naming her with a new identity of "mother of all the living."

A creation wrecked by curses leaves no one worthy, and no one deserves love, not even one. God is the only actor and provider of true love, underserved love, patient and kind, not envious or rude love. To hold on to a reality that doesn't play by the rules of deserving action—that is love.

Just as Hosea was given to love, just as Adam was given to love, just as Christ was given to love, sacrifice is true love. So God sacrificed His one and only Son for people who did not deserve, recognize, or want His love.

Love is made known by the action of Christ. He was killed for your transgressions, reconciling you to the Father, granting you His victory into eternal life. And you don't deserve it. That is love. Forgiveness when it doesn't mean that anything is fixed, grace and mercy when you know you didn't do the right thing—this is love.

Love doesn't always excite. Oftentimes it is the greatest challenge because we all just want connection fully and totally from spouse, lover, child, or friend. But we operate in a chopped, unfair, unfulfilling expression of love, always yearning for the greater completion. And so true love is an action. It is a sacrifice. The ultimate display of love is found in the gift of the good news of Jesus, God's Son.

And when one person forgives another, undeserved, unassuming, this is love. And it cannot be overcome because it is patient and kind, not envious or rude. It is forgiving, the ultimate act of love. But even if we cannot bring ourselves to love, that does not change the action of Christ. The end of the story is that He loves you, no matter where you have been or what you do.

> For while we were still weak, at the right time Christ died for the ungodly. God shows his love for us in that while we were still sinners, Christ died for us. (Romans 5:6–8)

You are restored to the eternal love and acceptance of the Creator. Now you are free to love anyone recklessly in this wasteland. You are already filled with the satisfaction of Christ's love that will never end. You are not afraid to expect that others will fail in the powerful struggle of relationship here and now. You will absolutely yearn for the perfect harmony of this patient, kind, forgiving, and true love. God has reframed your every expectation in love. And even now, in this dark valley of curses, be assured that He loves you by the sacrifice of His Son. And all will finally be made right. Undeserved love is freely given you so that you will have eternal life, and you are truly loved.

Unearned Thorns

There has been a garden in front of my bedroom window for as long as I could remember. Every morning I look out and see the beautiful fruits of my labor: pink flowers, a palm tree, geraniums, and mint. I love to smell the mint every morning when I crack the window.

But that garden does take work. I remember the mornings of digging and pruning just to enjoy its growth for a moment. And only a moment, until the first winter frost, and then my garden dies again. Every single leaf withered and rotted every year.

How do we spend our lives? Just attending a few fragile plants outside the window. Culturing, caring, feeding projects and people so that there would be something to enjoy. Just long enough until death do us part. All this work yielded bitter thorns and dead thistles eventually. Even though the mornings looked bright, the beautiful flowers don't last forever.

This is the common story of a garden and of life, tending the branches, signing the checks, feeding the roots, and dealing with the consequences. God's answer to Adam's disobedience in the Garden of Eden was, "Cursed is the ground because of you." Today, each of us feels the curse, not only within our own bodies but radiating also from the dying earth.

While it certainly seems far beyond our control, dealing with the cursed ground and a doomed world, God's promise for redemption of the whole earth is sure. And for us, God teaches us to find comfort the uncontrollable circumstances, the thorns and thistles, with honest words of lament and prayer.

*****

A surprising crystal clean morning after a sleepless night's rest, hints of fresh green life laced his deep breath awake. *Smells like life,* Hank thought. He could trace that inhale down into his belly, filling up his soul, spilling into his fingertips and the edges of his brain. It can't get any better than this, a good morning.

The sun wasn't up yet. He wanted to sneak out before anyone else heard him. Ever so silently, Hank made it to the bathroom without stepping over the creaky spot on the bedroom floor. A quick change into running pants and sneakers without even turning on the light, he then closed the door quietly behind him.

Purple dawns always inspired his hope, before the glaring sun of the day, before the rest of the world awakened, before the colors were too vibrant, before the cars rushed by to school, before his phone started ringing. Hank could breathe and think and run and sweat and think when he could get out alone, when things had the potential to make the most sense. And today he was nonsensically hopeful.

The morning felt good. He could see the near future. He was excited for the future a little further off. Once overwhelmed by the meaningless tasks of the monotonous days, he had been able to inspire others to take some of that off of his plate. Maybe he would have time to focus on the things he loved to do, not the things that were slowly killing him.

He couldn't get over how wonderful the spring air felt inside his head, breathing in, tasting every flower and the soil, warmed by little songs of little birds. This morning was something of a celebration, a surprise celebration, because he had not expected to feel so invigorated and alive after a night like last night.

Nights were complex. Harder. Darker. Memories. Worries. Regrets. Yesterday was another day that lasted too long. He almost lost it. It was close to being completely over. A most awful realization plagued his heart and mind. He was lying about what he wanted out of life. Well, at least it was changing. In one respect, he wanted to rule a kingdom. In another respect, he wanted to give it all up and pursue art and leisure. He wanted to dominate every woman that he's ever desired. And yet he wanted to be a righteous, strong man, swayed by none.

Last night, Hank had the most terrifying vision. He was sitting at his desk, covered in files and messages and documents. His well-ordered days were chaotically spread before him. Too many words that he couldn't control were spilling out from every direction. Hank was not a control freak, but it bothered him deeply to see all of his work laid out, confounded, misunderstood, in a messy pile. In real life, most everything was lost in some invisible iCloud, searchable of course, but he didn't have to directly confront the layers of unintelligible disorganization, like last night.

He couldn't remember if he had worked late again or if it was some sort of hazy vision from the gods or a recessed memory of his early days, in that small cubicle back in South Carolina. But he could still hear the papers shift under his frantic fingers. He could smell the crisp manila fresh out of the box. The stale-vacuumed taste sat on the back of his tongue, which he would rather not have tasted at all. He always hated that about the office.

Sitting there in the familiar chair that he formerly thought of as his throne, his heart beat louder and faster, thumping in his brain behind his eyes and ears. He could have ignored it if the pulse was anywhere else—his leg, his neck, his arm. But it was the painful drumbeat of his racing brain and his panic colliding into a single rhythm. He felt his neck tighten, jaw tension. Unreleased and unrealized wonderings overtook his breathing, caught like a fish drowning in oxygen. So much to breathe all around him, but his lungs would not access the air, just beating and gulping and squeezing and sucking in cement.

That's what it felt like, inhaling gravel, dulling his senses, brick and mortar pressing too hard inside his chest. All the while, his heart beat sped up to an insane pace. The heavy dark feeling restricted the air so much that he was feeling dizzy, gasping, tingling, on the edge of hysteria.

I'm going to die, Hank thought. *My heart can't keep this up. I feel like my insides are going to explode, or I will suffocate,* which made him panic all the more.

It didn't hurt, not really, that he couldn't breathe. It made him feel blank, as if his life was being erased by a great, creative director, snuffing out his work, his today, his legacy, his vitality, his vision, his mental awareness. He was being scraped off into the abyss.

Everything he had poured into this life, every hopeful seed, every minute, was choking out into the nothing. It didn't matter that he had spent his whole life working for what had been sprawled out onto his desk. And what was this? It was nothing more than a mass of fire kindling, papers memos, meaningless words. A career that held him hostage to want more, to do more, it was never going to end. He felt the flimsy dead paper between his flesh and blood fingers. Hank was feeling it. None of this would endure.

Suffocating chest pains melted into a subtle ache in his chest, in his throat. Death didn't scare him, if this was life. But even so, Hank wasn't ready to die.

And this vision, or nightmare, or whatever it was, inspired a forgotten regret that he hadn't given himself time to explore during the busy breath-filled moments of the everyday paperwork. This was not where he wanted to stop everything, giving his last minutes to perfectly typed briefs, worrying over declarative words about people he never touched or saw or even knew their name. How did he get here? Was this life's work worth the immanent death he was about to die?

So it was revealed. He was lying to himself and maybe to everyone around him that this was enough, that this was a fulfilling and meaningful way to tend a life. And it sunk down under his belly, down beneath the parts that he thought he used to know. And it was revealed that he longed for a ridiculous passion, for connection, for success, for domination, for vulnerable submission, for a garden to grow. And it was revealed that the papers and folders and meetings and appointments, they were just putting it all off until tomorrow, unsuccessfully soothing the searing pain, staying the full surrender, binding up his leap toward salvation.

Hank saw his death: heart failure, tired life, quiet end. Would anyone even cry? Maybe his wife would. Or maybe she would be happy to be rid of him.

Hank saw it, and it was not a question of if. It was when. How long would it take to die by unfulfilled monotony? How long would it take to play out all the righteousness of should and would and could? And was any of that even worth it? Could he change the course of good and evil for the sake of an unfulfilled desire?

Hank saw it. He had planted and tended a garden of nothing. Immediately, he wanted to run away from it all. There was so much more to life that he was missing, that he couldn't just give up on. Not now. Hank wondered, *What was meaningful? What was his ultimate purpose? What was important, really, in this life?*

Planning and putting in the long hours for the last twenty-five years. It turned out just as fruitful as the lost years of college, getting drunk behind the corner of a liquor store. Gone were his dreams of passion. Work, productivity, getting ahead, and making ends meet became the ultimate goal. Hopes of saying the truth, being famous, and creating a masterpiece all faded into oblivion over the too-short quarter of a century. But there was nothing new. And time was always too short.

His loss of creativity bothered him the most. Hank valued his artistic expression and used to think it would flourish into his greatest achievement. But now, that's where he felt the pain of too late and not enough. Instead, he was a good provider. Instead, he was a good leader. He could construct meaning in productive things other than passion and emotion. Those things, he had learned, weren't to be trusted to flourish anything valuable. And he was much more sensible than that these days. Even if his painting let him periodically dabble in that release, it just didn't make sense to invest that much time and effort there. He was a grown-ass man now.

If he were to paint, just paint, he would make no money at all. As much as he loved to swipe the brush over a blank watery canvas, he already knew that it would be a life of waste and poverty. There was no retirement plan for an artist. No one would want to buy his paintings, as good as he knew they were. People were generally happy with Pottery Barn, mass-produced media for their walls—no soul, no beauty, no meaning, just some accent colors that happen to match the throw pillows. *Give the people what they want, and you will make a living,* he thought. Hank didn't know if he could live with that philosophy. He actually despised it.

Alone in his office, he debated between opening the bottom-drawer bottle of scotch or scrolling through his private screening of pleasure. Something, anything, to distract him from the blood squeezing away from his chest. Something to shoot up some life or dull the angst in this midnight prison. For the next twenty minutes or so, Hank lost himself in the dark. Flashing flesh, erotic buzz, flooding euphoric high, silence.

Just over an hour later, he had locked the front door of his home and fell into his own bed next to his rigid, snoring wife. Sweaty undershirt, he slid his hand over her cold thigh. He thought about praying to God, but he couldn't concentrate. Dark. Ashamed. Still feeling the fingertips of death around his throat. Hank again swallowed the urge to escape, afraid of the end of his life and the empty harvest that was materializing, staring at the barren landscape on the dark room ceiling and seeing no way out. There was nothing to do about this.

Hank didn't know when he fell asleep again. The time dripped like molasses on the clock, watching the minutes. Twenty-three… twenty-four… But eventually, his eyes stopped seeing. His breath gave way. And finally, he was overtaken by the night, only to wake up, to forget, forced to attend the same suffocating gardens all over again.

It's not enough to know that he did his best. It's not helpful to hear where he did his worst. He was tending the tasks at hand as meaningful as he knew how. He had to make decisions, and they didn't work. Good or bad, the seeds he had sewn refused and rejected to grow. His vocations withered into silence. He lived among sinners, choked out by the weeds, overwhelmed, and unable to do anything to change the course of the world. Yet he will be held accountable to repent of the consequences.

The time, energy, and years he put into the growth of meaning and purpose only yielded sour grapes. What is the point? He wanted to scream it from the rooftops, but who would listen? And should anyone listen to the unhinged whining from a beaten, unsuccessful man?

It makes sense that God would punish someone for abandoning his duties, for doing the wrong things, for taking advantage of unappreciated blessings. Like a vineyard, overrun by weeds, one should pay the consequences of blessings unattended, untrimmed, uncared, forgotten. That makes sense.

But what about the times when he did his best? When he put in the time and sacrifice for a better world? When he was faithful in spite of faithlessness? Even that doesn't fix the situations of life, whether deserved or undeserved. A garden of thorns doesn't tell one what to do next. More often than he would like to admit, there is a meaninglessness that cannot be controlled. But he can't quite admit that. He would rather declare responsibility that there must be something to do. Because just complaining about it won't fix anything.

What can he do when he realizes that he has no ability to change the outcome? Does Hank really deserve to live this kind of life that is constantly marked by disappointment and failure? And what does that mean about his ultimate relationship with a God who ordains all things? How can a good God still submit His beloved creatures to constant suffering and struggle? What can he say to the Almighty One who has all the control but will not work it for Hank's good?

He had prayed to God to take the sadness away, to subdue the shame, to help him see the blessings around him, to fix what was wrong, to amend his attitude and outlook, to teach him how to live differently so he didn't have to grow into more failures. But to make it worse, God didn't have anything to say back.

He had prayed to God because he couldn't move. He couldn't endure. He didn't want to anymore. He couldn't work it out. All of the advice fell on lame feet and mute lips. Simple, they say. Just do it. Be the person you were before. Be the stronger man in the face of loss. Do the right thing. Do more. Pick up where you left off. Just stop feeling sorry for yourself.

They were right. He knew that. And he tried once more to praise God. He tried to listen to God to make it better, to fix the sadness.

Yet Hank didn't find anything good left to pray.

*****

This curse afflicts all of mankind: decay, destruction, unending labor, and a struggle with meaningless work. Positive thoughts and endless attempts do not relieve the angst. Dreams and high ambitions haunt and tease. The well-plotted future does not always materialize. And then, sometimes it's bright. The path through life teeters on the edge of excitement and unfairness. Often there is no rhyme or reason to why our good intentions may just fail and die.

But when something finally crumbles—be it a person, a life, a job, a relationship—we have the chance to see our internal lack of power to bring it back, to resurrect, to make it grow again. Cursed from the Garden of Eden, the world, the creation, our efforts will eventually prove to be unfruitful. This is a piece of the curse from the very beginning of the story. Man and woman were forewarned that their hard work would yield dead thorns and thistles from their endless labor.

> Cursed is the ground because of you; in pain you shall eat of it all the days of your life, thorns and thistles it shall bring forth for you. (Genesis 3:17–18)

Cursed is the ground, and to dust you shall return. It all is an empire of dirt. Build it, play with it for a while, but then it will blow away. We will spend most of our lives cultivating "important things" that will not yield what we want.

But it is not okay that a dream dies, that a life changes, that a love leaves, that a zeal withers. It is not okay that the virtue is despised, that the good is forgotten, that the ignored was the important. It is not okay that the repentant hear only silence, that the evil receive the blessings, that meaning can suddenly turn meaningless.

It is not okay that men and women work entirely too hard and do not receive just payment for their action. It is not okay that one must sweat and waste life on things that will not endure. The garden that is planted will still not give the fruit that is desired. The modern creation is also cursed. It is not good that we struggle on a dying earth like this.

But in times like this, we are overwhelmed with the curses. When dealing with the world outside of us, we realize it is beyond our ability to change or heal the greater reality around us. We learn we are not God, rather we are His creatures. We learn that we are subject to wind and waves, earthquakes and death. But in the face of this uncontrolled, cursed reality, God wants us to pray, scream, yell, and complain about these things to Him.

Prayers to God do not have to sound like clean and tidy praises, only thanking Him for the good. They do not always end with confident expectation. They do not have to impress and inspire us to clean up and sit up straight. Prayers to God can just as well be messy, unfinished, conflicted, raw, complaints to an absent Heavenly Father.

When we edit our speech in the context of our prayers to God, the devil smiles far below the clouds because by lying to ourselves about this broken creation, we are willfully conspiring with him to hide the truth. When we are quiet about the things that destroy and shatter, they continue to destroy and shatter us. Hiding our complaint from God confesses that He cannot touch it or that He cannot bear it, as if He doesn't already know about His cursed creation.

Thanksgiving, requests, and praise are only a fraction of life, especially when everything turns quickly to an unexpected direction, when the pressure is too much, and the complaint is too great for our remedies. These are the prayers that should not be shushed. These quieted prayers will hide us away from the truth. These unsaid prayers will devour our faith and trust in a good and gracious God.

The faithful servants of God pray in a way that address the most raw and hurtful parts of life, not just for the times when life is going well, not just for the times when God is clearly shown as the one to be praised. But we are trapped in the punishment inflicted upon the earth. Prayers like this in the Bible teach us to vocalize the frustration, anger, and lament to God about His unfair world.

And why would we not want to say these things out loud? We might admit something terrible about our life. We might admit something terrible about God who allows these things to happen. But these words should be spoken when our life doesn't satisfy. We can tell God that His promise and His blessing didn't work. We can hold God accountable to His words and promises. The history of faithful prayers seems to do it over and over again.

> How Long, O Lord? Will you forget me forever? How long will you hide your face from me?
> How long must I take counsel in my soul and have sorrow in my heart all the day?
> How long shall my enemy be exalted over me?
> Consider and answer me, O Lord my God.
> Light up my eyes, lest I sleep the sleep of death,
> Lest my enemy say, "I have prevailed over him"
> Lest my foes rejoice because I am shaken.
> (Psalm 13:1–4)

How long, O Lord, will You punish a man for working hard? How long, O Lord, will You allow arbitrary pain and sin and loss to attack him? How long, O Lord, do we have to deal?

He did the best he could. She didn't know what she was doing. It was a tough situation. It's not his or her fault. But it is too easy to make excuses. This will add and subtract every good deed and misstep to teach the next generation. You will pass judgments, offer more unfollowable rules, and sow the seeds of disappointment for yet another day.

How long, O Lord?

In another time, in another place, David lay in the dark, unable to eat, unwilling to move. Terrible weights pressed into his chest, as if the air was made of mud, and the dust of the cold, hard ground scratched in the inside of his nostrils. There was no way out of this. He couldn't think of anything to say, anything to do, shriveling in a corner, dried up, poured out, cracking.

It was quiet, unusually so, because they were all afraid to tell him. The clanks of the servants had been hushed. The voices of the children had been scattered away. It was an echo of nothing that rang in his ears, too loud to make any sense of it, pounding blank noise that told him nothing. No one wanted to tell him the boy was dead, but the silence answered everything.

It was exactly what should have been expected in the face of such exposed evil and disobedience: punishment, death, and destruction, yielding nothing but thorns and thistles. But the thing was, he didn't realize this future belonged to him until it was just too late. Hindsight made everything clearer, and yet the insight gained was irreversible.

He thought of the beautiful woman Bathsheba. He thought of the tiny infant life he held when wheezing away his last breaths. He thought of the ecstatic joy, having planted a new life with this woman and child whom he loved. But now crouched in his vomit, cheek resting in the dirt, having been punished for the sins within, and the sins without, it had all spun out of control.

David, king of Israel, was no stranger to incredible pain, unanswerable questions, unmatched and unconquerable sin. He was great and mighty, a successful man of Israel who murdered, lied, and stole. Yet he was under the illusion that his kingdom could transcend the curses, that he would be able to grow and prosper in his own reality. But in sorrow, he was enlightened. There was no escape from the curse of sin, from the curse of his unavoidable dying garden.

But not only unfruitful endeavors but also punishment of death and repayment followed his family to the very end. He was a good king of Israel breaking the commands of God, enduring the curse for grasping the meaningless, choosing death, just as everyone does from the beginning of all things. He was following in the footsteps of his ancient father, Adam; mother, Eve; experiencing the fallen and broken world, whether it was done to him, done by him, followed through by the horror of the curses that would follow him the rest of his life. He was taking up the death that was proclaimed to every man, every woman, the product of their existence walking through the wilderness of thorns and thistles.

> Cursed is the ground because of you; in pain you shall eat of it all the days of your life, thorns and thistles it shall bring forth for you. (Genesis 3:17–18)

Could he have? Should he have? These are not the questions. Go back, and do it over. There is no going back. Avoid the evil. Overcome the grave. One way or another, everyone is caught in the sickening realization. You have sinned. You fall short. Your work, good and bad, will end up in vain. It was all for nothing. And you are traveling closer to your return to the dust.

King David was familiar with complaint… *I have sinned. I am sorry. There are things I know, and I don't know. They are yours. What can I do now? Deserved or not, I am cursed. Realized or not, I am cursed. Confessed or not, I am cursed.*

And sometimes, God remains silent. How long, O Lord, will You forget me? Will you hide from me when I finally have the breath to pray, and you do not answer me? What am I supposed to do with that?

How long will I take counsel in my own heart? Because God is quiet. Because I am defeated. To whom shall I go? When I stay in my own head, when I stay in the failures and triumphs of my own heart, all I can find is a sinful failure, someone who was not effective, someone whose job will come to an end. How do I pray that to the God who created such a disappointing creature, a disappointing creation?

How long, O Lord, will Your creation not work with me? How long will I be blamed for sin that is mine and also blamed for sin I cannot control? How long will You stay away? How long will death win?

How long, O Lord, will You teach me that everything ends up meaningless? Whether I kept Your righteous rules or broke them. Whether I sacrificed my life for those who could not protect themselves or kept my life for myself—what is the difference? It didn't work. Why have I given everything to just reap failure?

How long, O Lord, do I have to pretend that I love Your righteous rules? When they have left me wanting. When I paid my dues, which You righteously ordain, and You didn't return my love, when I kept Your covenant, and You kept silent, I did everything I could to follow You, and I am still found guilty. I fell far, far away, and I could never make it back.

How long, O Lord, will my failure be my story? I reap the downfalls of my own life. I deal with the downfalls of my children. I open and pay the bills, as my beloveds starve me of dignity and respect. I work until exhaustion, while the mess towers higher over my head. I run faster, drive farther, even though it is all falling apart with every mile logged on the odometer.

How long, Oh Lord?

Our prayer of "how long" confesses the depths of faith. First of all, it is truth that the world and our lives are messed up, beyond repair. Second, it is a cry to the only one who can save us, who could possibly fix it, a complete dependence on the Almighty. Third, a lament is an expectation. It is a hope that the world and this pain will not be the end and there is more to come. "How long" is a truthful, expectant, and painfully trusting prayer.

> But I have trusted in your steadfast love;
> my heart shall rejoice in your salvation. (Psalm 13:5)

"But I have trusted," prayed David, complaining to God in this psalm. Despite everything he saw, everything he'd done, everything unfair and justified, despite the advice and consult from the depths of his heart, he has trusted in God's merciful love.

This is an absolutely bold and ridiculous statement, that one would trust in something outside of himself. Mankind is born into selfishness and bred to trust our own judgment and feelings and rationality and emotion, cultured creatures who have been encouraged by the world that their own direction reigns supreme. And so naturally, in the face of failure from what God says we should do, then His laws become in conflict with our own. So we must define and realize and admit where our prayers and trust is centered.

A lament, a complaint to God, is a faithful conversation with God. In the shadowed corner, at the end of our rope, we have to admit that we cannot take comfort in our own heart and soul. We do not have the answers. And even if we think we have answers, sometimes the truth does not work like we think it should. Sometimes God does not show up like we think He should. Sometimes we are devastated to learn that the right way, the law of God, does not turn us into better people. The right way, more often than not, shows us the horrible sinner that we have always been. Sometimes we see the horror of our world, our society, and absence of control over our lives. And we can admit the reality outside of us that has beaten us down.

So living in the midst of a curse, do we simply look inside? Do we assume our part is to make it work? Shall we trust in our own god of intellect, discipline, and our own soothing comfort?

Or do we sing with David, counting on the steadfast love of God? Do we look, with the heroes of prayer and suffering to the mercy of God? Those who patiently waited to be saved from the slavery bond in Egypt. Those who wandered and were preserved in the desert. Those who prayed for salvation even though life was unfruitful.

It's all right to question, cry, and complain, to despair that the bill required is unfair, to call a thing what it is. You have failed. The right way doesn't always work. This world is beyond our ability to heal. People are outside of our control. God is taking too long. It's all right to pray that.

It's all right to admit that you have failed, to pick apart the times when you should have been stronger, better, more intelligent, more compassionate. It's all right to be mad at the rules—the laws that don't always yield success, the laws that don't give life to those who follow, the rules that only have the power to condemn terribly, completely, the rules that made you realize that you are the problem or that you cannot escape the meaninglessness. It's all right to pray that.

And this lament to God is a freeing prayer. When you admit that you have a salvation that is outside of your own actions, outside of your own will, outside of your own heart, it sets you free from the rules. The love of God is shown by the sacrifice of His Son, not the sacrifice of your life. Because you can't save yourself. You can't get rid of the terrible things in this world that threaten. You can't destroy the terrible things in themselves that hurt and hinder. You can't purify the hearts of our own growing and wayward children. You can't save the world. And how could you be honest enough to rejoice in another salvation unless you prayed like this, that your action, love, intellect, will not make everything all right? You cannot do it. You will fail. You are not enough. Sin really hurts. Death really kills, and this world isn't getting any better. You can happily admit it all. You can, in full confidence, lament.

> But I have trusted in your steadfast love;
> my heart shall rejoice in your salvation. (Psalm 13:5)

But instead of persisting in despair, we rejoice in a salvation that breaks into our sad, confused reality. We trust in an answer that is the same, whether we are good or not. We have a God who is faithful to us, even though we are not. And we can admit this uncomfortable truth that we are ignorant, ineffective, and foolish. These are the people who God loves. These are the people who rejoice in a salvation, one that is not their own doing. These are the people to whom God has given the gift of everlasting life, who believe in the sacrifice of His Son.

The steadfast love of God refers to the ridiculous, sacrificial love that God endures for His people over and over again. When His first man and woman broke His heart in the Garden, God mercifully revealed that an offspring of the woman would crush Satan's lying head. When the people of God were enslaved to generations of slavery and poverty in Egypt, God miraculously peeled apart an ocean for their victorious escape. When His people complained and lamented in a barren desert, God mercifully fed them bread from heaven and poured forth water from rocks. God has a history of steadfast, merciful love, especially in response to the lament of His people.

But it was not just for the ancient nation of Israel. In a manger, in a stable, God sent His one and only Son. From the eternal throne of heaven, God's Son descended into flesh, hunger, bruises, sadness, blood, and pain. God sent His Son for the healing of the undeserving nations, for the redemption of ignorant and bad people, for the salvation that should not have been given. But this is the steadfast love of God. At the same time, it is the answer to the truthful laments, the answers that we cannot come up with on our own.

Trusting in the steadfast love of God is trusting in a wisdom and an action that is not your own. Trusting the steadfast love of God is believing that Christ did enough on the cross to redeem every bad decision, outcome, or reality you have seen yet. Trusting in the steadfast love of God allows us to endure the unfruitfulness of our own gardens. It allows us to rejoice and hope, especially when we fail.

> I will sing to the LORD,
> because he has dealt bountifully with me. (Psalm 13:6)

And while we lament, we sing. While we are broken into pieces, admitting, and learning more in the valley of the shadow of death, we are comforted. While we faithfully complain, trying to survive in a dying garden, we trust in a salvation and an answer that is not our own. The Lord has dealt bountifully with even me, in the midst of a suffocating world of curses. Despite our own bondage to the desires of our heart while we are still sinners and suffering under sin, the Lord has declared us to be victorious through the death and resurrection of Jesus.

Our perspective does not always match the perspective of the Almighty God. Our short-term lack and comfort is not the end. Thorns and thistles are not the end of the story, of our story. We faithfully lament and complain, both honest to our circumstance and honest about the enduring promise of God. Caught in a cursed existence, we are at the same time caught up in Christ. His bountiful blessings of life and salvation will outlive every sin, every tear, every challenge, and death itself. All will finally be bountiful, fruitful, and productive as it was promised. As it should be.

More Than You Can Handle

I remember the night I had my first panic attack. It was almost midnight, and I was desperately trying to close my exhausted eyes. But my newborn baby was forty-three miles away, barely breathing in the neonatal intensive care unit (NICU). The doctors made me go home; there was no room at the inn. But my four-day-old newborn could not yet survive on her own. So she stayed in the hospital without me.

Where was my baby? Was she breathing? I couldn't feel her skin. As a mother, the natural instincts of survival kicked in. And my system couldn't handle it. Gasping for breath, my heart was bursting out of my chest. This was more than I could handle, and my body was physically agreeing with me.

It is a fantasy to believe that God will not give us more than we can handle. It's part of the package. God proclaimed the curse to Adam as consequence for his sin, *"You are dust, and to dust you shall return."* Death, returning to the dust, is the ultimate curse that cannot be avoided, and that is definitely more than anyone can handle. But He has mercy on us all. God also feeds us and sustains us through this valley of darkness. And God loves us by His Son, Jesus, handling everything on the cross for us!

*****

A man shouldn't feel this way, he told himself. Stabbing pain inside, he wished it was an actual knife and not this invisible dread. *A man should die on the battlefield honorably by a sword or a gunshot wound,* he thought as he looked at the haunting digits on the wall clock, *not here on a couch, by a pit of emptiness. That's not how a man like me should go down.*

Tom just wanted to punch something hard, so hard that his hand would bleed and his knuckles would split. The caged tension made his body rigid with an uncontrollable desire to release it. But at the same time, he couldn't move. So angry that it rendered him paralyzed, so frustrated with the uncontrollable situation that he was at a loss of where to even rest his eyes, He didn't have the strength to care about anything, let alone do anything.

It was only the second afternoon since he buried her, less than thirty-two hours after watching the pieces of dead earth hiding her under the ground. They shoveled, but they didn't see what Tom saw. Her pretty blond hair closed up in that box. He had to watch the manure of the earth, swallow her soft fingers. He knew they were painted lavender from holding her limp hand for hours before they wheeled her body away down the sterile hallway. He hadn't really comprehended that her familiar hand, that hand that fit into his palm effortlessly for more years than he should remember, would be completely untouchable for the rest of his life while he lived on this earth without her.

And it didn't feel like a piece of him was missing like they said it should. This felt like he was being ran over by a truck. In slow motion, he was fixed to stare at the dark and dingy underside, pinned under the tire, under the surface, unable to get up. Piles of dirt invisibly absorbed the air. It was only the second day, and his muscles, brain, and bone were already decaying with hers in a different world. How could this possibly get any better when he can only remember how good it once was? It was the good he didn't know he had. Before he realized, it was goodbye, and a new unchangeable tomorrow had dawned without warning.

Tom tried to remember what today should have been like. Busy at home, dropping off groceries, she was losing her keys always. He was complaining about the long hours at the office, and she giggled when he made fun of the fence next door. They should be sitting on the porch in the early evenings, deciding where their next adventure would take them, whether it was to Vegas or their Friday night pub. Damn. He would have to tell the guys at the pub. He would have to say why he came without her. That is, if he could ever go back.

He didn't think about that until just this moment. Who would Tom have to tell that his wife died? Who would be in need of his comfort and strength? Who would offer their shallow empathy? They would all say their cliché I'm so sorrys. But he knew it wouldn't really change their day. And on Friday, they would all still go to the pub with or without them. They would continue to relax with a glass of whiskey, laughing at Brian the bartender's jokes. But Tom would never again be able to relax like that. Would he laugh? He probably wouldn't ever go back to the pub, would he?

A man shouldn't feel like this, the pressure of expressing these feelings. That crap is not going to bring her back. It will not atone for the petty fights they had last week for which he never asked for forgiveness, for which he was always too proud. Feelings, of any kind, will not hold off the aggressive empathizers. They only care about their own sorrow. They don't really want to hear about his. A man needs a path. He needs an honorable direction, not just an emotional dump. Yet Tom couldn't see the path. He couldn't conceive what was next. And he couldn't move.

Tom had heard stories of those who had lost their spouse, of course, but he didn't ever consider that he would be one of them. So suddenly, his world had collapsed. Even though she wasn't his whole world, everything had changed. Tom spent a healthy amount of time away, and maybe it was too much time investing in other projects, hobbies, and flirtations, hindsight of guilty memories. Tom's spine unconsciously shuddered, and a dart of bile shot upward in his throat.

Such a waste of the time he had with her. He never stopped to think that he would be suddenly thrown out of the simple, comfortable, taken-for-granted world they had cultivated over the last twenty-seven years. He never imagined this aching desire to feel the warmth of another single human body, even two days later that he was beginning to forget.

And it wasn't unusual. It wasn't unheard of. That someone dies too young. That someone watches their life as they know it destroyed in a second of time. But this was more than he could handle. Tom was going over the edge. This was not handled. And Tom was not going to just be okay. Without a doubt, he knew that.

So what then? At the end of the conversation, what now with his life? He tried to recall the snippets of Instagram wisdom that scrolled through his brain. The little sentences plastered over the stoic pictures. Thirty-second reels of advice passionately performed catchy quotes by important people, much more important that he probably would ever end up to be, the little words that taught him how to move forward. Think better. Live better. If only his distracted mind could always remember. If only those words worked, those stupid empty words. If they even worked, they would want him to pull himself out of this funk and somehow find strength, be a man, fight through to his own death, not be dissuaded by such a setback. Why did he care so much anyway? How could he let something, anything, anyone affect him so deeply? Where would he find the drive to go on? It definitely was not inside of him. He was exhausted, not only from caring but from caring that he cared. It was all too much.

Maybe this was an incredible wake-up call that he had cosmically screwed up beyond repair. Maybe the little sins added up, and this finally was his punishment. Maybe God was unusually angry at him and left him here in the in this wilderness to suffer alone. But this was just too much to handle.

*****

We groan and scream for our expectation lost. Sometimes we didn't even know we were operating with such a high expectation of reality, until we are in mourning for what should have been. The whole creation does this, not just sad disappointed people. Because the creation—the trees, rocks, sea, and birds—were not created by God for destruction and decay. God made His world to live forever. God made His people to live forever. Yet God's people chose death and destruction for themselves and for the earth they walk upon.

> And to Adam he said, "By the sweat of your face you shall eat bread, till you return to the ground, for out of it you were taken; for you are dust, and to dust you shall return." (Genesis 3:17, 19)

"You will not surely die," said the lying serpent. "You will surely die," answered the Creator of all. Consequences spun out of control, and man and woman experienced much more than they could handle. From dust Adam was made completely by the creative hand of God. From dust he then and now returns completely by the righteous hand of God. Mankind received death for their disobedience.

Before this, however, man and woman enjoyed a life that they did not choose for themselves, a gift that was given to them. The consequences for their sin resulted in a reality that was out of their control—death and a return to the dust. The punishment from God in which the man and woman now walk is more than they can handle.

Yet you have heard it said that God will not give anyone more than they can handle, that somehow, believing in God means that He will protect from all suffering and pain. Mistakenly, it is concluded that one should be able to handle it all: move mountains, avoid suffering. Then you will know you are on the right track. Yet suffering is a common theme for the faithful people of God, even for His one and only beloved Son. God exposes our weaknesses by suffering. He acknowledges our disappointing and dying world by our experience with suffering. And right here, He often gives you more than you can handle.

Suffering is commonly thought of as the greatest evil, especially a suffering that you cannot escape. A life-changing alteration in perception forces you to ask questions you never thought you would have to ask or even were important. Suffering compels you to seek answers that you may not have previously been prepared to hear. Suffering invites you to peek behind the curtain of unexamined comfort. You can take a look at what is failing, what does not endure, what is not working. You eventually must embrace the reality of this finite life. You can see the reality of the cursed world. And in suffering, you can feel with every sigh that this is not right. This is not how it should be. This revelation in itself is a gift of truth. The overwhelming lack of control is good awareness of the current state of this world.

Suffering is the unanticipated consequence of a broken world because we were created with the knowledge of what should be. So every time that we feel that aching awe for what is not, those are the times in which the suffering of the curse overtakes. All is laid out bare.

And yet suffering is the way that God may turn you to Him, the end of your rope, with nowhere else to turn. And there is the God who will do it all for you. But sometimes it takes you to the very bottom of existence before you can see the need for salvation. You need to despair of everything that you have to give everything that you held tightly to that is not His. You do this so that He is the actor of mercy for all of you, not just the parts you know are lacking, even the parts that you think are pretty great. God's plan to destroy you actually helps you because that's when you can recognize salvation is completely up to Him.

> For God has consigned all to disobedience,
> that he may have mercy on all. (Romans 11:32)

God reveals that we are not the gods of our own destiny. We are not the creators of lasting and enduring happiness. We are not the Almighty Creator; rather we are beggars, every one of us. When the cursed story of the external world traps us in the dirt, when the shortfalls of our deadly confidence is shown to be nothing but shifting sand, that's when we can simply admit that this is all more than we can handle.

The truth is, every one of us totally and completely needs a Savior. God is faithful, and He will give you more than you can handle so that your own solutions and your own paths to salvation will be crushed. Your own illusions that you are the god of your own universe must eventually be tried for what they really are. Your identity in the things you can create or have built for yourself must be held accountable to the identity that our Lord has already given you. We are all burdened with more than we can handle so that we remember where life and salvation truly reside. God gives you more than you can handle so that you have nothing left but to remember He is faithful.

Yet the road through suffering is terrifying and draining.

Elijah was tired of running, of caring, of worrying. He was just so tired. And the broom tree was the only place he could find to rest. But it wasn't real rest. He just couldn't move anymore. The journey had been too long. It all had been too much.

> Elijah was afraid and ran for his life. When he came to Beersheba in Judah, he left his servant there, while he himself went a day's journey into the wilderness. He came to a broom bush, sat down under it and prayed that he might die. "I have had enough, Lord," he said. "Take my life; I am no better than my ancestors." Then he lay down under the bush and fell asleep. (1 Kings 19:3–5)

Exhausted, dry mouth, and out of breath, tasting the raw dirt in his cheek—it wasn't worth the effort of another step. He had been faithful. He did what God wanted at every turn, but it didn't matter. He tried to follow the good and faithful path, and it even worked for a while. But not anymore. It was out of control. He was hunted and could not find his way back. Death was the only way out. He knew that now. And he just needed to stop everything.

The people after his life wouldn't give up; they wouldn't give in. He used to think that he wouldn't ever give in, especially with the

Lord on his side. Moving mountains, conquering anything, that's how this should go. He even had experience with incredible success in the past. The Lord is great. And He should prosper in everything, right? Especially when sent on behalf of the Lord.

Afraid, running for his life, worried that he had nothing left to give, meaning and purpose sapped from his bones. What used to propel him forward was now absent, gone, sucking the strength and will from the innermost place.

"I am no better," Elijah admitted to himself, "than those who went before me." Once he was confident that the Lord had chosen him, molded him, made him into a man who could sustain in such a dire situation. But, no, he was just as vulnerable as all the prophets that went before. He was just as weak as widow and the orphans that he was sent to strengthen. He was overthrown by the wicked, despite the promises he thought he believed.

It was too late. He failed. He was done. And the journey was so much longer than he could go.

This great prophet of God was given more than he could handle. It is a sobering reality for each and every follower that God may allow this to happen. Let us fall beneath the surface. Let us experience an exhaustion and desperation beyond our control. Let us slip into a sleep from which we cannot pull ourselves out.

He will give us more than we can handle. He will allow us to suffer. It's not outside of a faithful relationship with God. And He is still good. And we are still loved.

> All at once an angel touched him and said, "Get up and eat." He looked around, and there by his head was some bread baked over hot coals, and a jar of water. He ate and drank and then lay down again. (1 Kings 19:5–6)

Elijah woke up, hurting, sore, still tired, and probably angry because nothing was different. His situation in life hadn't changed. And the temporary rest he had found for himself was irrationally and rudely interrupted by God. But contrary to what we've been taught to expect, Elijah didn't overcome. He didn't get a second wind nor draw on the power from within. It was, in fact, too much for him to handle. Rather he was asleep, removed, dead. God didn't leave His prophet alone. Pestering God, who chased after His people like a stalker, the Angel of the Lord woke Elijah up. He struck him, punched him, touched him to the point of torture.

God allowed this situation to get so bad that Elijah could not recover on his own account. To make matters worse, God sent a messenger to violently beat him awake. God stirred His servant from the sleep of death. What a strange God to permit such sorrow and inflict such pain, kicking a man when he was down, beating his eyes wide open, even after Elijah had finally fell into some rest.

God will likewise give you more than you can handle. God has given many of the saints before you more than they can handle. But He hadn't left them alone, and He doesn't leave you alone, not at all. And many times, it gets worse before it gets better. Just when you think you see the bottom, you may have to go deeper, and darker. He may even send a messenger to beat you awake, making sure that you don't fall asleep and forget.

But even this wasn't enough to inspire Elijah back to action because He laid back down. Eat, drink, and it still was too much.

How often do you lie back down after receiving the gifts that should propel you forward, after learning that your trial and trouble are not too much for the Lord that He will sustain you despite your doubts and failed efforts? This is the way. Just trust in the Lord. But what happens when we cannot, when we are too tired, when the journey is too much? Have we failed the test, that we couldn't sustain ourselves? Or did He fail us?

> The angel of the Lord came back a second time and touched him and said, "Get up and eat, for the journey is too much for you." So he got up and ate and drank. Strengthened by that food, he traveled forty days and forty nights until he reached Horeb, the mountain of God. There he

went into a cave and spent the night. (1 Kings 19:7–9)

"Get up and eat," said this angel. With no hope left in his own being, Elijah did what the angel said. And yet, this messenger from God didn't bid him to work, to do more, to keep going on the strength that was clearly lacking. No. Rather the angel of the Lord fed him. Bread was miraculously given from the same type of coals that sucker punched Isaiah in the mouth (Isaiah 6:7). God has a habit of cleansing His servant with pain. In Isaiah, the angel of the Lord cleansed Isaiah's guilty lips so that he could continue to be in the presence of God. Here, there, in history, and present, God acts when it is too much to be handled.

Always, God shows Himself to be faithful, aggressively faithful, more than you want, absolutely more than you deserve but exactly what you need. Elijah lay down, yet God came back. You lie down, and the Savior is lifted up.

He overwhelms you with your disobedience and unending wandering. He awakens you to the death you have earned. But God pierces the hands and feet of His own suffocating Son. And ever since, He touches your lips, ears, eyes, and heart with a new life forward, again and again, saying, "The journey is too much for you. I have given you more than you could handle. Eat. Drink."

This is what God habitually gives His people: a journey that they cannot complete by their own strength, by their own reason. Without Him, there is nothing He needs from you. By now, hopefully you have realized you have nothing to give to Him except brokenness and tiredness and ineffectiveness.

Like Elijah, the people of God struggle to stay awake: prophets, disciples, even you. In the Garden of Gethsemane, when the disciples should have been awake as Jesus prayed His last prayers, instead they slept. In the middle of his prophetic journey for God, Elijah slept. In the middle of your confusing and sorrowful walk, even you now sleep. But God won't let you settle for that incomplete rest.

The angel of the Lord comes back a second time.

This journey is too much for you, giving words to what we all knew finally but words we were too afraid to admit. This journey is too much. You are not strong enough. You are not good enough. You won't be able to find your way out of this mess. You are not able to make this journey. You can only fall asleep because it's too much.

Again, Elijah got up, ate, and drank. He was continually strengthened, even though he didn't deserve it, even though he couldn't stay awake or do enough. God returns, and He feeds His people again and again.

His food was enough to propel and sustain His people in the wilderness. Forty days and forty nights, Elijah wandered all the way to the mountain of God. God made sure that he made it, even though it was more than he could handle.

And you can expect that you will be given more from a God who loves you, when even a beloved prophet of God, Elijah, was given more to the point of exhaustion, when even the beloved Son of God, Jesus Christ, was given more to the point of a shameful death. It is more common that God gives His beloveds more than they could ever handle, pressed out into a wilderness, beyond the comfortable garden of bounty—more, too much, but never beyond the reach of God.

More than you can handle will claw to the surface in every place, in every vocation, in every position in life. It will haunt you in the dark. It will hover over your days. It reminds you that the dust of destruction waits. When God gives you more than you can handle, He is showing you who you are: pitifully overwhelmed, a beggar for mercy. To dust you shall return, no matter how great you thought you were. But when God gives you more than you can handle, God is also showing you who He is, unrelenting in faithfulness, especially in the times and places when you don't deserve it, always when you cannot handle it.

More than you can handle is the way God will draw you to Him. When you have nothing left, there is only one Savior. You can't pretend anymore that you will be okay. You are finally confessing the truth that you were not created to make it on your own. You are desperately falling away, drifting off.

Like Elijah, that's when God slaps His children back to reality. Like Elijah, He wakes you. He feeds you. He sustains you so that you will keep walking through the wilderness. God gives you more than you can handle to bring you back to life. "God consigns all to disobedience so that he may have mercy on us all." You have only begun to learn that God's tiny mercies, His hidden food, His simple Word are more powerful than your greatest efforts will ever be.

But the worst enemy, the last enemy, death, still returns God's creatures to the dust from where they were formed. "You are dust, and to dust you shall return." This is the ultimate curse, and there is no way to handle it. Only God could make such a change to His entire creation. Only God could make sure that dust and death would not be a problem, since the man and woman must die.

Yet in the same breath that man and woman were condemned to eternal sleep, God promised a taste of life. After the announcement of the curse of death, "to dust you shall return," Adam turned to the wretched woman, his partner that was also about to die. He looked at the crumbling creature, remembered something critical that God had said to the serpent, and he called her something else. In the middle of their "more than they could handle," man and woman tasted the promise of God. Her name swirled around his mouth and tumbled over his lips. Sweet and delicious, Adam called his wife, Eve, meaning "the mother of all the living."

At the right time, while His people stood before Him in dirty shame, the promise of life was fed to ears and heart: *You will not die ultimately, Eve. You are the mother of all the living. You will not die, Adam. The coming child will overcome every shadow of too much to handle*. In fact, the promised offspring will reverse death itself. A promised offspring of God would crush the head of the serpent. The promised offspring would overthrow the curse of death and dust. This was the life promised to the mother Eve.

The opposite tensions of too much to handle and freely given nourishment define today's struggling, striving people of God because the journey is too much. And even God's people cannot muster strength from within. As much as we believe that the Word of God gives power, it doesn't always make life any easier for us. We still live in the middle of a cursed reality. We walk outside of the Garden, surrounded with only promises of what it was like and what it could be. When life becomes too much, we might conclude that there is something terribly wrong with our faith or our relationship with God.

And, in fact, we are right. There is something incredibly wrong. We walk in sin and death, and that separates us from what we were created to be and rejoice in. We walk in sin and death because that is the world that has been handed to us as well. We participate in the evil that is not what was intended. And we are constantly overwhelmed by the wilderness that was not intended to be our reality. But here we are, walking in the wilderness.

However, there is food. We pray to God, "give us this day our daily bread," when we are the smallest of children until we are advanced in years. Give us this day our daily bread. God gave it to all of us, whether we deserve it or not. God gives daily bread, even without our prayer, to all wicked, evil, and ungrateful men. But we all pray in this petition of the Lord's Prayer that God would lead us to know it and to receive our daily bread with thanksgiving. Yet what is meant by daily bread? Martin Luther expounded, "Everything that belongs to the support and wants of the body, such as meat, drink, clothing, shoes, house, homestead, field, cattle, money, goods, a pious spouse, pious children, pious servants, pious and faithful magistrates, good government, good weather, peace, health, discipline, honor, good friends, faithful neighbors, and the like."

And so there is food; there is drink. God's gifts will sustain in every trial and need. Even more, there is food and drink in the community of the Christian church. Given and shed, we share a heavenly bread, an answer from the Almighty God, forgiveness from Christ and a reason to go on when there is no reason within oneself. This is the sustenance that Elijah received. This bread kept him awake, moved him forward, even though the reality and wilderness didn't change. God's mercy is not ever earned nor deserved, but it is fed to the suffering wanderers in the wilderness.

Those of us who are given more than we can handle, there is bread from God that sustains us in the wilderness. This is a food that is entirely received. There is no way anyone could have earned or created such a sustenance to make it through. "God consigns all to disobedience so that he may have mercy on us all." All are made disobedient by His word so that He may entirely feed you, especially when we need it the most. Because we are disobedient and weak, needy and beggars, broken and hungry, overwhelmed and sleeping.

This is the right time that Christ died for the ungodly. The right time to entirely give freedom through forgiveness. The right time to give life when death reigns freely. The right time to reconcile enemies to God and sustain them with the body and blood of the One who came to save. It is more than you can handle. Yet God is happy to sustain and fulfill you. Those of us who have recognized that we are wandering in a cursed creation of more than we can handle, we have begun to understand the great wisdom that hides beneath suffering. God desires to be your entire answer, beginning to end, in wilderness and paradise, from dust to eternal life.

Wisdom, Not What You Thought

It is fulfilling to pass on wisdom to the young and curious. And the wisdom of God carries a great invigorating power—that is, until you have that hard conversation beyond the solution of conventional wisdom. I had that realization during the talk with a girl from our youth group. She was only fifteen and just found out she was pregnant. Of course she loved him. Of course she wanted to do the right thing. But a whole world of hardship and judgment had suddenly appeared for her.

Wisdom that would make it all right was beyond her reach. Words of wisdom that would soften her consequences were beyond me. However, we both took comfort in God's wisdom, which was made for that moment. Finally, we faced up to the only hope we had left—the wisdom of God found in Christ, outside of our own action and knowledge.

The curses we have experienced in our self, in our relationships, and in our world taunt us to fix them. Even Christian advice found in the Bible may have us believe that we can resolve the problems of the world. But God's wisdom gives life through a tree, and it is not the wisdom that we thought.

*****

Two fifty-two. She could make it eight more minutes, her armpits sticky. There was a pit in her stomach. *Just don't look up.* She was pressing a chipped pink nail deeper into her pencil, making neat little moon-shaped divots up and down the yellow paint. *Look at the pencil, not the people.* She didn't want to catch anyone's eye, not for eight more minutes.

A pretty little female voice was ticking on, talking on, saying more and more, but she couldn't follow. She lost this train of thought a while ago. But everyone else sitting there seemed to be totally engrossed, leaning forward on the couch, cradling crafted coffees, and nodding expectantly at each other—well, except for Stephanie. *Good. Just keep talking. Seven more to go.*

She knew some of the girls here, not very well, more of a few acquaintances that she had gathered over the years. But it was enough to finally get her to come. Some of these ladies have been friends for a long time, playdates at the park, soccer camp carpools. But she had never known them quite like this.

"Once, I read this: She makes bed coverings for herself, her clothing is fine linen and purple… And I have been quilting and making their clothes ever since," finished the sweet blond mama with a sleeping infant bound in cloth, wrapped on to her chest.

Steph let out an involuntary sigh. She didn't mean to. It was great that this ancient saying was all the inspiration a busy mother needed to start quilting and making her own clothes. God, what else did she do? It was likely she told us every single amazing thing that she did because that was the way this evening was going. Luckily, no one paid any attention to the quiet exasperation from the side of the room. It seemed as if the other ladies were getting a bit restless as well. Maybe she wasn't the only one after all.

Duped into believing this was a Bible study that would solve some of her problems, Stephanie felt so much worse now by the end of the hour, excited a bit by the caffeine later than needed and exhausted by the insufficient roller coaster that she had just experienced. This Bible study on Proverbs made her realize one thing for sure: She was certainly failing at being a woman, failing at life, and generally failing at being a good person.

Her friend, Maya, offered to end them in a prayer. *Thank goodness,* thought Stephanie, *I need to get out of here.*

"God, I just want to thank You for everything. Your word is so good, and it shows us Your plan for our lives. Help us to follow Your rules and commands so that we will be perfect in Your sight. Amen."

Confirmations of amens and smiles radiated throughout the room, and Stephanie felt trapped. Although the heavy air began to lift as cups shifted and purses appeared from the couch edges. Fresh air, she needed fresh air. No more of these fake conversations because now she knew what they were really thinking. The tiny hints of condescension or pity, those sideways glances that she couldn't quite place before—now she knew from where they stemmed. Tonight she had been invited to the sacred table of the ones who did it right. And she was not invited as the guest of honor, as if they had something to learn from her. No, she was there so they could teach her their godly discernment, God's way to live from the Bible.

Heaven knows she wanted to do something that worked. Divorced for about four years now, it wasn't any easier. It all seemed like the right thing to do at the time. The fighting was unbearable. He wouldn't ever listen to her. She had given up listening to him. It was a mess that just wasn't working, and she had reasoned that this was better for the kids. Happy mom, happy dad, separate places—but they weren't happy. At least she wasn't. It turned out to be worse. Money was tight, communication between them was strained and even more uncomfortable, and now the kids were taking advantage of both of them to get exactly what they wanted. Life had spun out of control, and she didn't know what to do.

She knew she was wrong. She knew she had chosen badly. But now what? Could she go back? And would it work out any differently?

They were sweet, her friends, she knew that. This was the only way they knew how to try and help her: discipline, accountability, a pathway through her mistakes. It all makes good sense, and she appreciated them for that. But there was a huge unforgiving elephant that hangs over her head when they talked to her, when she remembered her messed up choices, when she couldn't escape from the guilt and regret that drowned her with every word, every condemning word from this "helpful" Bible study.

Maybe if she had learned some of this advice earlier, she could have done it all better. Maybe if she had better friends or a better ex-husband, she could have avoided this failure. Maybe if she could control her temper and her tongue, everything would be okay. But even if she began today and changed it all around, could it wash away the past? Even if she followed the wisdom advice to the letter, could she keep it up ever and always?

Finally slipping out the front door as everyone was hugging their goodbyes, a blast of cold air cleared the chatter in her brain for a second. *I don't know if I can do all that*, she wondered as honestly as she could. And that made her incredibly sad because she already knew it would be too much.

*****

The rights and wrongs, the "do this, and you will live," the proverbs that our grandmothers could recite and have been passed on from generation to generation—these are the words from God that if we could just follow them, if we could just keep them, then we would be okay. These are the parts of the Bible that make the most sense, practically speaking: Ten Commandments, laws of God, righteous people doing certain things for the most righteous God, the wicked inciting heavenly punishment, pain and suffering for those who don't follow the way of the Lord, discipline for those who won't love the Lord God with all their heart, soul, and mind.

This is the law of God that condemns and accuses and demands righteousness. The law of God is good and perfect, just and right. There is no disputing what He has said is good. He is the author and Creator of everything in the universe, and He has actually defined what is good. The wisdom found in Scripture originates from this goodness of God. The wisdom of God is the foundation for life and breath to everything. This wisdom, literature from the mouth of God, is found in Job, Psalms, Proverbs, and Song of Solomon. Most commonly though, we hear many snippets of wisdom from the book of Proverbs.

Almost every Christian has had the opportunity to experience at least a few proverbs from the Bible in their own immediate life. Whether it's a calendar page or a coffee cup, these quotes have come across as the most basic wisdom from God: how to live, conduct, and prosper in life.

We crave a deeper wisdom to succeed and endure this life. It's who we are, whether we look to self-help, meditation, other religions, or the Almighty God. We are created for this lost wisdom that we once had in the Garden. Proverbs is exactly the Word of God that we should want to study. It is wisdom literature in the greater context of the Bible, a genre to its own, not a narrative or apocalyptic but songs, verses, and poems about the wisdom of God. It offers quick and easy sayings about everything from family to finances, anger to love, catchy quotes that have been easy to memorize to take a bit of wisdom with you throughout your life. It is no wonder so many Bible studies hover around the book of Proverbs, imparting wisdom to the young and old, simple and wise.

> Blessed is the one who finds wisdom, and the one who gets understanding,
> for the gain from her is better than gain from silver and her profit better than gold.
> She is more precious than jewels, and nothing you desire can compare with her.
> Long life is in her right hand; in her left hand are riches and honor.
> Her ways are ways of pleasantness, and all her paths are peace.
> She is a tree of life to those who lay hold of her; those who hold her fast are called blessed. (Proverbs 3:13–18)

A beautiful image of God's wisdom is the tree of life. And as the Proverb says, those who find wisdom, those who get her, those who lay hold of her, those who hold fast are called blessed. In Proverbs, the way to the tree of life is spelled out. In Proverbs, we meet wisdom, the way of righteousness, life, and blessings. In Proverbs, we begin to see the hidden path from the beginning, the forbidden fruit taken from the tree of knowledge restored to the eternal fruit from the lost tree of life.

> Hear, and accept my words, that the years of your life may be many.
> I have taught you the way of wisdom; I have led you in the paths of uprightness.
> When you walk, your step will not be hampered, and if you run, you will not stumble.
> Keep hold of instruction; do not let go; guard her, for she is your life.
> Do not enter the path of the wicked, and do not walk in the way of the evil.
> Avoid it; do not go on it; turn away from it and pass on. (Proverbs 4:10–15)

Upon reading Proverbs, the path should become clear. Righteousness can be defined. The way of the foolish was wickedness and violence. There are no gray areas; you are either for God or against Him, listening and following His command or not. And so, reading the wisdom of Proverbs, it is too tempting to think you can simply choose the right path. All you need to do is walk in the right direction, know the things to avoid, to make yourself better in life. It seems simple if you are willing to walk the walk, not just practical earthly wisdom but a godly advice from above. It boasts to be life for those who follow and death for those who turn away. Take to heart the warnings of this wisdom, watching every step you take. According to its word, wisdom should lead you right back to the lost tree of life.

> But the path of the righteous is like the light of dawn, which shines brighter and brighter until full day.

> The way of the wicked is like deep darkness; they do not know over what they stumble.
>
> My son, be attentive to my words; incline your ear to my sayings.
>
> Let them not escape from your sight; keep them within your heart.
>
> For they are life to those who find them, and healing to all their flesh.
>
> Keep your heart with all vigilance, for from it flow the springs of life.
>
> Put away from you crooked speech, and put devious talk far from you.
>
> Let your eyes look directly forward, and your gaze be straight before you.
>
> Ponder the path of your feet; then all your ways will be sure.
>
> Do not swerve to the right or to the left; turn your foot away from evil. (Proverbs 4:18–27)

The book of Proverbs seems to spell out the path of salvation. The wisdom of God found in this book grants life and death. There are things that must be done. Once you hear, you do it. You hear the call of wisdom, and you follow it. If you are foolish enough not to listen, you are excluded. You're out. Maybe you were never really there to begin with.

This path leads you to make you worthy of the tree of life. Adam and Eve chose the wrong path, and they were cut off from the tree of life in the beginning. But is it possible that any knowledge can lead you to life, the right knowledge that if you follow the words in Proverbs, then you will grasp life? If so, this means you cannot play the fool. You must avoid the things that lead away from the tree, learning from the mistakes of the first humans, so nothing you do will sever your relationship with God. And are you able to do such a task?

> Then the Lord God said, "Behold, the man has become like one of us in knowing good and

> evil. Now, lest he reach out his hand and take also of the tree of life and eat, and live forever"—therefore the LORD God sent him out from the garden of Eden to work the ground from which he was taken. He drove out the man, and at the east of the garden of Eden he placed the cherubim and a flaming sword that turned every way to guard the way to the tree of life. (Genesis 3:22–24)

Man and woman were cut off from this tree of life, the true wisdom, but now they were nourished by a tree of knowledge of good and evil. This tainted knowledge now led them to a new reality. The creatures of the Almighty now choked on sin and pain and death. The way to life was guarded. The path was hidden as the tree of life vanished from their reach, so far away that now they could only hear about it from a distance.

Every day, man and woman were reminded of a promise about that tree, eating to have eternal life. But that was not their reality right now. It was promised that a Savior would come to make their path straight again. But for now, mankind must walk a long, hard, exhausting, deadly path. We all must bear the consequence of a cursed world on the outside of the Garden, blocked from the fruit of the tree of life. And all we have is the hope and reminder of such a tree.

And here is where you are walking right now, in between the tree of knowledge and the tree of life, stumbling along the way, trusting that the blessed tree is waiting for us at the end. It seems so very far away, and it is even too far to see with our eyes. But our ears still hear the promise as we continually seek to find the true way.

Yet do you wonder, what is this path that you are on right now? How do you know that you are really walking the right way? Do you ever wonder, what if your steps stumble? Do you ever worry, what if the way begins looking dark and gloomy? Maybe it was never on the way to the life-giving tree in the first place. Have you been a fool this whole time? What is necessary to walk the right path? Are you fulfilling your purpose? The more you learn about wisdom, the right path, and the wrong one, the possibility arises that you are wrong.

We learn from the paths of the wisdom of Proverbs that there is a right and wrong way to go. Yet we seem to choose the wrong way most of the time. Why did God block the way to the tree of life? Because He knew. He saw. Adam and Eve bound themselves in sin and death in a world of curse. And we, too, are bound to choose the sinful darkness that lurks in our hearts and minds. Just because there is exhortation and encouragement and threats to do the right thing, that doesn't mean we have the ability to do the right thing.

"That by the words of the law man is admonished and taught, not what he can do, but what he ought to do; that is that he may know his sin, not that he may believe that he has any strength… I confront you with the words of Paul: 'By the law is knowledge of sin'—not power of will!" Martin Luther wrote in *Bondage of the Will* about the power of law and the power of our will. The tree of knowledge has brought just that, our knowledge of failure, yet not the ability to do anything about it or to change our situation.

So our path in righteousness looks so very different than we first imagined. We cannot achieve the righteousness by following good advice and reenacting words of wisdom. Rather, our journey to restore the tree of life from the Garden of Eden is just another impossible grasp at salvation.

A journey with and through Proverbs marches us closer and closer to that tree of life. At first glance, it's not the one we expected. Twisted and tangled, a tree is planted right in the middle of the law of God, rooted in the righteous wisdom of Proverbs. The path we are walking inches us closer and closer to the tree of life. But it is not righteous advice that we must follow, lest we fall out of the favor of God. It is not the law of the faithful that must be finished by the believer now that he has a wisdom from above. No, our path in Proverbs is a tree of life that drips with the blood of a Savior, that you will eat from once again.

> Then the angel showed me the river of the water of life, bright as crystal, flowing from the throne of God and of the Lamb through the middle of the street of the city; also, on either side

> of the river, the tree of life with its twelve kinds of fruit, yielding its fruit each month. The leaves of the tree were for the healing of the nations. (Revelation 22:1–2)

Here, our twisted, dusty journey ends at the tree of life. In Revelation, the end of the great story we began in the Garden, we hear about a picture of the new heavens and the new earth. In the city of Jerusalem, the people of God are centered around this tree. It is placed in the center of the city where God and the Lamb are on the throne. The water of life flows from the center, where the tree is rooted. The center of God's people and worship in the new creation is this tree of life—twelve fruits, twelve tribes, twelve disciples, fruits of the gospel feeding the thousands, healing all who take and eat. Here, at the end of our journey, the tree of life is the gift of a risen Savior, a victorious Lamb, bountifully producing, healing, and life everlasting.

This is our hope of life eternal. This is our comfort in our Lord Jesus Christ, both now and at the end of the race, the place where we will sit in the shade together, rest and relax, looking back over the hard journey to the end. Relieved that we made it, joyful that the strife is over—it's such a comfort to consider that tree. No more walking. No more pain. No more hunger. No more fear. Restored to eat from the tree of life that had been lost since the beginning, our hope lies with the risen and crucified Savior on the tree of forgiveness. Tree to tree, from Genesis to Revelation, one must pass through the tree of blood, sacrifice, and salvation. And this is the wisdom of God.

This wisdom is the path to salvation. But it turns out, it's not your path to walk. It is not your journey to take. Just as the story from the tree of life began with a promise, it goes through Proverbs with a promise and ends with the promise fulfilled. The story from tree to tree does not feature you choosing the right path. The righteous path belongs to the One who was born of God and born of

Mary. The story of your journey from the tree of knowledge to tree of life had to go through a tree of death, which you could never do.

> He himself bore our sins in his body on the tree, that we might die to sin and live to righteousness. By his wounds you have been healed. (1 Peter 2:24)

Christ kept the way of Proverbs and then chose your path of torture on that tree. Christ redeemed us from the curse of the law. Christ chose the tree of death, the good and righteous tree of justice that stands in the middle of Proverbs. Christ bore your wicked sin, bled and died for your foolish disobedience, hung cursed and dead for you. He did this in the midst of Proverbs, in the midst of wisdom, in the midst of a curse. And His undeserved death on that tree restored your path to the tree of life. By His wounds, you have been healed. By His blood, you can take, eat of the tree given for you. By His death on the tree of the cross, you have life.

Then what of these proverbs, this understanding, these laws of God, if they don't always make you into a better person? Then what is the purpose? Is it just random vanity inflicted on God's children as a joke? What about the woman who followed the wise ways her whole life, yet loses everything? What about the wicked unbeliever who takes centerstage and receives honor and beauty and riches and life? Do we simply write it off, making up a story of retributive justice to follow them later? What about the situations that are entirely unfair? What if righteousness is so far gone that we can't repair it? What if we admitted our efforts were not always fruitful, no matter how hard we worked? What if we admitted that our success and advantages appeared by dumb luck, not wise choices? Then what is the purpose of wisdom and knowledge?

Job said what he should have said. He did what he needed to do. Every other time in his life, everything worked out just fine. And he wasn't used to this feeling, this sickness, this awful depression that weighed like betrayal. He did it all right, and it didn't work out at all.

It was only midmorning, and his servants had run into his bedroom with the devastating news: collapsed house, dead children, assets destroyed. At every turn, there was another insane and underserved consequence. It was a personal pandemic of resources, comfort, and a blow to his ego, not that he was egotistic at all. Every morning, he gave thanks to the Almighty God that he could continue in this part of the county, that his children were safe, that he was made for this place and time and purpose. He was well aware of his moral failings. He was well aware that he did not do the things that he should do to sustain this sort of incredibly blessed lifestyle. He was a good servant of the Almighty—well, until this morning anyway.

But this hurt a little too much because he was so careful with his cattle, with his words, with his eyes. He learned the words of wisdom so very well, and he put them into practice better than his neighbors, better than his wife, better than his children. No, this wasn't a "who is better" game. He loved the law of the Lord, and it had proven to serve him well thus far.

Reflective guy that he was, he knew that it wasn't anyone else's fault. Yet he also knew he didn't really do anything wrong. He knew the knowledge was supposed to give him life, and it wasn't working, at least not this morning. But he had done everything the exactly right way according to the wisdom of God. That should mean something.

Soon he began to itch just below his armpit, and then his waist, his skin uncomfortable, burning, as if the physical smell of burnt landscape was not enough to make him sick. He couldn't stop itching. Boils, blisters, puffing and swelling—his body was heaving and reacting. It was pulsing and on fire, with a pain he had never felt before. What was this life? He was physically, mentally, bodily destroyed.

Finally, he dared to ask. Who was this God who allowed such pain to overtake him? The God Job worshipped, where was He? When his children were dead and his body now bled with sores, who was this God that was supposed to protect him even after every good thing was turned into death and dust? What did He really know about anything anyway?

In a world of curses, the right path and the wrong path may prove to be interchangeable, the good are brought low, and the wicked are exalted. Everybody and nobody gets what they want. It doesn't work. This wisdom doesn't always make productive and happy people.

Sometimes it appears as if the wisdom of God is a joke. It only helps those who help themselves. When the rubber hits the road, we need this wisdom to work out of our benefit for our good. The wisdom of God, praying and hoping and wishing, that's for the suckers who still believe in fairies.

So for Job, he had very real questions about the wisdom of God because he endured the pain until the end. He did not pull back. He did not try to do something different. He pushed the wisdom of God, which led him to understand the suffering under the righteousness of a hidden God, which led him to trust only in the mercy of God's promises. And this is the beginning of wisdom. Job could not do anything to change this situation. Job had to trust only and solely on the wisdom of the Lord.

This is the beginning of wisdom. There is nothing you can do.

> Fear of the Lord is the beginning of knowledge. (Proverbs 1:7)

And wisdom has nothing to do with figuring it out. The wisdom is not producing your own righteousness. Wisdom is not following the impossible law of an Almighty God, even if you know and understand the path of good and evil. Even that cannot gain you the tree of life. The wisdom of God is Christ crucified, the tree of life planted in the midst of every good proverb. The wisdom of God is your path to the tree of eternal life.

St. Paul writes,

> "For since, in the wisdom of God, the world did not know God through wisdom. It pleased God through the folly of what we preach to save those who believe. For Jews demand signs, and

> Greeks seek wisdom… But we preach Christ crucified. Christ, the power of God, and the wisdom of God" (1 Corinthians 1:21–24).

The folly of the world is exposed. It is cursed and dying. The folly of our hearts and minds are realized. We are weak and dishonorable. The folly of our ability to do what God requires is laid bare. We are poor, miserable sinners. We justly fear the wrath and judgment of God in circumstance and action. The wisdom of God is not a simple prescription to turn around a bad day. It was before the beginning of the earth. The wisdom of God is the speaking and the spoken. The wisdom of God is a Word of God incarnate, hung on a tree, crucified on a cross for the forgiveness of all sin. But from the beginning, Christ crucified remains the merciful wisdom of God given for us.

In fact, a misunderstanding of this wisdom can hinder your path to life. When you try to figure everything out, when you try to make a plan for your salvation, that is when you are taking wisdom into your own hands. That is when you are trying to be God himself, satisfying the righteousness required to win His love and acceptance. That is when you lose the path. That is when you lose your creatureliness. That is when you attempt once again to become greater than the Almighty God in law and obedience.

Jesus Christ took complete responsibility for you, your misunderstanding and inability to be what God made you to be, your inescapable crumbling empires of dirt that you were placed into, your lack of life, because you will die without access to the tree of life.

We rejoice with the depressed and beaten, foolish and cursed. Christ crucified restores us all to the lost tree of eternal life. He is the wisdom that ultimately solved the problems we struggle with. Trusting in the promise of God with Adam, Eve, Job, and Stephanie, we know that things are set right only by the wisdom of God: Christ crucified. Even though our knowledge is flawed, and everything around us is dying, the Almighty wisdom assures that this curse has been finished.

Only One Thing Matters

These stories have been melded from the lives of many people I've met, but they have been written for my own reminder and consolation. As a mother who has struggled to love all of her children, as a wife who has tried to live up to every good thing that was expected, one day it all crashed under the pressure of these curses. Every piece of this unforgiving reality beat me down, taunting me, overtaking me. And I learned well that I had nothing left in myself to fight back.

I had nothing but one thing. With every failed effort, every angry word, every death, every missed opportunity, and disappointment, there was hope. But not at all in myself, or my strength, or my resolve. When everything was stripped away, I saw so very clearly; there was only one thing that mattered. My fervent wish is that you will allow yourself to see this naked reality so that you can also see the only thing that really matters.

*****

This was all wrong. She never really envisioned the future but always assumed they would all be sitting next to her on a Sunday morning. Today, however, Hannah noticed the long, empty pew, where not one of her children was sitting. She didn't have to reach over anyone to get a hymnal, didn't have to move her legs back and forth as they shuffled by to go to the bathroom. It was quiet, even though everything in church sounded exactly the same.

Her children were old enough now to make their own decisions. Apparently, Sunday morning wasn't high on the priority list in contrast to late night parties, jobs, and young families. Even though all of her children still lived in town, a few still in rooms in her house, they had slipped out of the routine of going to church. Over the years, one by one, more important matters of life had finally left her alone in worship this morning.

The familiar seats, brown worn cushions, this was where Hannah raised most of her family on shushes and cheerios. This was the same upholstery from twenty years ago. She recognized the scratches in the wooded pew armrest from her son's fascination with her keys when he was about four. Now he was twenty, and God only knows where he was this morning.

Today she was sitting here, alone, ashamed. She was left to remember all of the times when she could have done better: brought them more, taught them more, been there more. She didn't realize they might leave the church, the faith. She didn't know if they believed. Yet Hannah had no idea what to do about that now.

She had watched the other parents deal with their children leaving the nest, leaving the church. Her friends, whom she had raised children with, all turned into the same story: Their kids disappeared. They grew up and decided not to come back. She wanted to believe it was the way of the modern culture, that a generational gap made this church irrelevant to the faith. Because too many young ones, she watched them walk away into the darkness.

It was funny but not really at all: the pride that Hannah used to have, the high opinion of her parenting, of her family. She had overcome many obstacles to get to this point—well, to get to a point. Looking around her this morning, she envisioned it very differently. She always thought she would be the one who beat the inevitable story of ending up alone at church.

In the years past, Hannah tried not to look too long at the women who were sitting in solitude while the church bells rang. If she did, she began to imagine how they possibly ended up there, how they made the wrong turn or bad decision so that their family ended up somewhere else. She tried not to make up the stories of how she would defeat all the temptations, how she had already overcome the proverbial bumps in the road. Time had passed, and she suddenly realized her Sunday morning looked no different from the ones she pitied her whole life.

Face-to-face with a ghost that had tortured her from the inside out, seeing the shadowed version of herself that she carefully despised in the eyes of her desolate brothers and sisters every week. Finally, Hannah recognized that veiled stranger she tried to ignore in their eyes, in herself.

She was no better than the generations who went before.

She didn't figure it out.

The organ began to play a familiar song. What was it? It broke in and distracted her from the quiet reflection of her hidden reality, snapping her back to where she stood in church, in worship. Here she was with brothers and sisters in Christ who helped her when she needed it, a community and a stronghold when life became crazy. It was no different today, whether she was here alone or back when she was here with her kids or, even longer ago, with her husband. What was that song? That made her remember things. What exactly was it even making her remember?

Each note inspired a rush of safety, warm blood, and relief. She felt rested and home, like a blanket that presses just enough on your skin for the calm. Through her ears, the notes pulsed softly in memory and real time.

This was the same feeling she could remember from when she held her son as a baby almost twenty years ago, and she could still feel the newborn heat cradled in her arms at night. When he would scream that tiny high-pitched cry in the black midnight, waking her from a dead, relaxed sleep, gently picking him up from his crib, rocking the rigid infant slowly, calmly, until there was a breath, a pause. Tiny muscles were melting to the rhythm of a mother's heartbeat. Fingers were caressing the fuzzy sleeper that held her baby boy as he fell back to sleep.

Remember this moment, Hannah would tell herself, memorizing the sounds and smells and a touch of time when it felt like it mattered, back when she tried. She could still feel that calm.

Sadness. Reflecting. Remembering. When her son was a baby. When her daughter was a toddler. Even as they grew through their awkward teenage years, she was always there. They were always here. Hannah was a mother who actively tried to be good at her job. And she thought, *in the end, it would have proven to be a job well done.* But here she sat, alone, responsible for her children's faith, and the lack thereof. What happened?

Yet there is no preparation for the shock when she might have the opportunity to perceive that her belief, her experience, her hope, her comfort had not solidified in the hearts of her children. She was surprised because before today, there was no doubt that it would transfer to them. And then it didn't, even when she tried to give it her best, especially if she gave it her all.

Now, also exposed by the unavoidable reality, she was finally ashamed. Now she sheepishly recalled the words, the stories when she assumed everyone else was doing it all wrong. Now she heard her reckless judgments imparted among those who walked next to her. Now she saw the audacity that her ignorance afforded her, elevating herself, standing in as the savior, pressing out the single hope that she was ironically proud to teach, deeply guilty.

Additionally, Hannah now knew that she was not just a failure to her own family. She had also been a selfish example to the hurting, the lonely, the sitting-alone-in-church people because deep down, she had believed that she was better. She thought she had figured out the secrets. She had never before identified with those lost and desperate people. Yet today the world she thought she knew pressed her into depths she never imagined.

*****

A large part of a parent's concern for their children includes their future, their belief system, moral standards, and what will be the most important concerns of their adult life. Therefore, continuation in a faith that guides and sustains is critical. Parents will not always be there to save, to teach, to give their children what they need. They must inspire their children to do this for themselves. When children grow into their own lives, it is necessary that they have their own moral compass, direction, and support system for their adult life.

The expectation is heavy, especially for the one who has put significant time and energy into one's own faith, which has guided and sustained through the worst of times, through the best of times, building an inheritance of sustenance, of sure-footed legacy given to the generations of the future that becomes one of the most precious gifts. This knowledge could live on eternally—passed along, offering direction and peace, no matter what the far reaches of life will throw out. Hope for more, even when the mentor has moved beyond. What better gift could you give to a child and to the future of the world?

All generations live under the curse of a defective world, the curse of failing children, the veiled struggle of good and evil, and the fear and taunting of death. Yet sometimes it is not clear that this is the world that exists or that this is the world in which we attempt to navigate. It is unbelievable, sometimes, that this creation has been poisoned by sin, along with every man, woman, and child. But it is necessary to see, to know, to understand when you must seek refuge.

It all began with only a few tiny drops from the heavens. Water that was meant to give life suddenly overflowed and filled the earth, smothering the life it was meant to sustain. But Noah and his family were chosen to outlive this disaster. His wife was not any more righteous or thoughtful than anyone else, but she would be the only mom to make it, skeptically nodding her head when her husband told her about the imminent flood, imagining the worst, pitying her friends who were moving toward certain death. Even if she didn't know exactly what would happen, she believed it was going to be something terrible. And maybe, just maybe, she had misunderstood her calm, peaceful life as a cosmic reward for a job well done. Maybe there was an entire reality of which she was not aware.

Then came the raining and the screaming.

Those outside the boat couldn't swim long enough.

That's when she knew it was for real. Everyone else realized a little too late.

Her too-nice neighbor, whom she always looked up to; her father, who taught her how to make lamb stew; her childhood best friend that kept the dirty secrets she never even admitted to God—they were drowning. And knowing herself, she didn't deserve this chance to live while they choked on the judgment of God. This was a judgment that she was not good enough to escape.

Her boys, with their wives, huddled in the corner, wide-eyed, surrounded by a miraculous menagerie. Stoic faces matched the steady hand of their father. Even though they were grown-ups, they couldn't hide that they were scared out of their mind, even while they floated safely in the ark.

Just last year, one of her sons had informed Noah and her that he thought he would be better off away from the family. He was growing up, moving on, and the prospect of choices in front of him were not looking good. His mother knew that he was involved with the wrong friends and possibly including the girls from the other tribe. He didn't offer the sacrifices with the family anymore, and she prayed that he was at least saying his prayers and would stay faithful to his young wife. But she was terrified of the truth. She was concerned about what he really believed. What would the future hold for her child? Noah had become so invested in the calling from God that he was not as present as he should've been in all of this heartache.

She was worried. She diligently raised her sons to have all the benefits of a life of faith. And one by one, in their own unique ways, they were questioning; they were sinning. They may have even been on the road to rejecting God forever. She even considered, by their confession and their actions, if they deserved to be drowned in the judgment flood. The flood happening right outside the sturdy walls of this boat.

Noah's family, eight souls in all, shuddered at the fatal revelation as the ark rocked through the waves. To escape this judgement of God, she realized that she wasn't good enough. Her boys weren't righteous enough. Even her husband, although God chose him for this incredible task, wasn't perfect. But there was something more than that for all of them. In the terror and safety of this flood, there was an ark. God had a plan that not one of them could have imagined nor could they have created it on their own. They had a chance at life when life was undeserved for all of them.

But here they were, protected from the most destructive flood storm of the world, in the ark, undeserving yet chosen.

God saw that Noah was a righteous man, but He never said anything about Noah's family. Noah's obedience and listening to God, his believing the Word for himself, counted him righteous. But it was not just for himself. God counted Noah's whole family righteous. And because of God's mercy, Noah's wife and his sons and their wives inherited life. Not because they were so righteous and amazing but because God chose them, so that a new creation would be able to flourish.

This is the grace of God. This is the core of the mercy of God, that even while we were still sinners, God pours out His grace on us. The ultimate event of God's great mercy was the death of His Son. Jesus gave Himself up to be pinned on the cross so that sinners could float free—sinners who didn't deserve to be remembered by His grace, sinners who had forgotten their prayers, even sinners who were trying to run away.

God remembered Noah and his family for life. They were not forgotten in the sea, in the storm, in the multitude, in the depths of death. God remembered because He promised that He would.

> But God remembered Noah and all the beasts and all the livestock that were with him in the ark. And God made a wind blow over the earth, and the waters subsided. (Genesis 8:1)

And God remembered then. But He also remembers even today. When He says something, He will do it. And it doesn't have much to do with the sinner who receives this blessing. The action begins and ends with God. He is the one who gives life and takes it away. And so we listen to His Word, and we trust His choices instead of relying on ourselves, incomplete failing sinners who do not deserve mercy.

However, an enemy of hope still whispers deceit. The evil one would have us not remember God's promises. The serpent from the Garden of Eden would rather we forget all about this curse so that we would forget about the cure. We cannot deny the visible change and decay of God's creation, the strife in our relationships with spouse and children, the products of thorns and thistles to repay for hard work, and certain death as punishment for sin. We cannot ignore the raging storms of our groaning world. But there is God's promise of resolution that was spoken from before a curse ever touched creation. The serpent was given a word of judgement, and we were given a promise of hope.

> I will put enmity between you and the woman, and between your offspring and her offspring; he shall bruise your head, and you shall bruise his heel. (Genesis 3:15)

This curse carried by the body and soul of the serpent relates to his final judgment. It's not going to work out very well for him, as the Son of woman is foretold to crush his head. The Son of God, born of Mary, is the promised One that will defeat the devil once and for all. Death will not be the final act. This is the promise that God gives to the serpent and woman and creation. This is the promise that Adam proclaimed by the name of his wife in the midst of a flood of curses, "mother of all the living."

The serpent's reign of death was promised an end. His head would be crushed. The havoc that he wrecked would be set right again by an offspring. The battle of good and evil would be won. God certainly remembered His promise to all mankind when He sent His Son to dwell in the flesh.

Likewise, the flood's kingdom of death was promised an end. Thunder and the lightening, pouring, swamping, overwhelming waters, anger and justice rain down from the heavens above. For forty days, Noah and his family, eight souls in all, endured the rain. Yet God remembered His promise. He remembered His people. He concluded the judgment with His sure salvation.

Finally, God promised there would be an end to all suffering under the curse: to man and woman and serpent, to the scared family on the ark, to all of us who wander through the valley of shadows, the valley of rain, the flood waters that never seem to recede. God has promised an end to the curse from the very beginning.

> The Lord said in his heart, "I will never again curse the ground because of man, for the intention of man's heart is evil from his youth. Neither will I ever again strike down every living creature as I have done. While the earth remains, seedtime and harvest, cold and heat, summer and winter, day and night, shall not cease." (Genesis 8:21–22)

God gives life. He wants life for His creation. So when the waters subsided, after death overtook all of creation, He made a new creation. He wants His people to live. He wants His people to multiply. He wants His people to be what He created them to be.

> The earth had dried out. Then God said to Noah, "Go out from the ark, you and your wife, and your sons and your sons' wives with you. Bring out with you every living thing that is with you of all flesh—birds and animals and every creeping thing that creeps on the earth—that they may swarm on the earth, and be fruitful and multiply on the earth." (Genesis 8:15–17)

> And God said, "This is the sign of the covenant that I make between me and you and every living creature that is with you, for all future generations: I have set my bow in the cloud, and it shall be a sign of the covenant between me and the earth. When I bring clouds over the earth and the bow is seen in the clouds, I will remember my

> covenant that is between me and you and every living creature of all flesh. And the waters shall never again become a flood to destroy all flesh. (Genesis 9:12–15)

Clearly, it is God who is in control. The story of past and present time is His story, holding back the waters, letting flow His anger, moving His people across the desert wilderness by fire and clouds, feeding them with heavenly manna. It is God who sends the storms and He who calms the sea. Wind and waves are in the palm of His hand. Suffering and too-long journeys are the result of our broken relationship with Him and this cursed world.

And clearly, God is in control: when He moves His hand of protection and salvation to save His people, when He builds an ark to keep His people safe, when He puts a bow in the sky so that His people will remember, that He will always remember. He will always remember them.

God continues to care for His people in this promise, preserving Noah and his family, saving God's people from Pharaoh, leading them through the wilderness, sending a Savior to heal broken bodies and hearts and souls, building a community of people in real time to confess and remind each other that Satan is defeated, the curses are resolved, and we have eternal life.

But it is a challenge to exist in a reality that is not entirely visible and only heard. It is a very hard thing to trust in a Word that you can't always see. And what if you wander? And what if the children don't hear? And what happens when you find yourself questioning the promises which you once knew to be true? Within yourself, you will only find instability and fear about who you are. You will have mistrust for the future. You will struggle when the times get hard, so much that you may break. To whom shall you go?

Where do you find safety and hope in this turbulent flooded-over world, of pain and suffering, of vanity and things that pass? Where is the hope that the answer still endures, even though everything in this reality passes away? The promise of the offspring, the promise of the rainbow, the promise of Eve all point to the only thing that really matters. The only thing that matters is the promise of eternal life that God has given from the beginning of all things, the life that was always intended for His creatures, the one that is put aside for you.

And He has promised that you will not live forever with the burden of your curse. He has promised that there is another who carried all the curse and sin and destruction with which you struggle. He has promised, before any curse touched the man and woman, that the head of the serpent, of death, would be crushed by a Child.

This curse was carried by a babe, born of a virgin. He took into His own flesh and blood the stench and decay of every human. This Son of the spirit bore the burden of every sin. He carried it all, heaving, dragging, bleeding, to a mountain set aside for the final consequence: death. Yet not lost in the ever-spinning timeline. This was the altar of redemption for all of humanity. God answers God. Christ sacrifices Himself. Forgiveness, life, and mercy belong to you on account of the one who carried it all.

On account of Him, you may see yourself a little too clearly. You have failed. You cannot carry your curse. Your path is not righteous, and you have made grave mistakes that will impact your own life and that of others. Your vocations are incomplete. Your purpose and meaning are lacking. You have been selfish, unbelieving people who have raised up another generation of sinners. When this loud and dying world overwhelms, God remembers. He provides a place where only one thing matters: a place to be assured of forgiveness, a place that is safe in the holy ark of the Christian faith.

The one thing that the devil despises is that you believe the Word of the Lord: forgiveness. He hates that you dwell in the place, with people, in the language, remembering the memories, living among the experiences of God's mercy. He wants you to forget who you really are, who you are created to be. From the beginning of the world, we have all grown up in sin. But those who believe also grow up in the promises of God, His protection, and mercy. Consider this prayer by Dr. Martin Luther that echoes our flood story and its implications for us as we wander in the wilderness:

> Almighty and eternal God, according to Your strict judgment You condemned the unbelieving world through the flood, yet according to Your great mercy You preserved believing Noah and his family, eight souls in all. You drowned hard-hearted Pharaoh and all his host in the Red Sea, yet led Your people Israel through the water on dry ground, prefiguring this washing of Your Holy Baptism. Through the Baptism in the Jordan of Your beloved Son, our Lord Jesus Christ, You sanctified and instituted all waters to be a blessed flood, and a lavish washing away of sin. We pray that You would behold Your child according to Your boundless mercy and bless him with true faith by the Holy Spirit that through this saving flood all sin in him which has been inherited from Adam and which he himself has committed since would be drowned and die. Grant that he be kept safe and secure in the holy ark of the Christian Church, being separated from the multitude of unbelievers and serving Your name at all times with a fervent spirit and a joyful hope, so that, with all believers in Your promise, he would be declared worthy of eternal life, through Jesus Christ, our Lord. (Luther's Flood Prayer)

The holy judgment flood buries us with Christ. The deadly cleansing waters drown every sin by virtue of the promised offspring of Eve. But just as Christ was raised from the dead, we too will walk in the newness of life. By a watery death in baptism, we are united to the One who has crushed the head of death. We are crucified, drowned, resurrected, and now free. We have been entombed in the ark, kept alive by God's mercy. We are defined by His everlasting promise.

> Do you not know that all of us who have been baptized into Christ Jesus were baptized into his death? We were buried therefore with him by baptism into death, in order that, just as Christ was raised from the dead by the glory of the Father, we too might walk in newness of life. Now if we have died with Christ, we believe that we will also live with him. We know that Christ, being raised from the dead, will never die again; death no longer has dominion over him. For the death he died he died to sin, once for all, but the life he lives he lives to God. So you also must consider yourselves dead to sin and alive to God in Christ Jesus. (Romans 6:3-4, 8–11)

And your curse is carried into a tomb. Death is paid. Consequences fulfilled. God is satisfied with this unblemished Lamb who takes the sin of the world away. God answers God. He wakes from death alive and victorious. Christ destroys the paradigm. Christ rewrites reality. Your sentence has been served, and life is the end of the story because He has done it. Christ has given salvation graciously and mercifully to you.

This is the only thing that matters.

Take comfort, you who are gathered in the ark of God's salvation, where you were washed and cleansed in baptism, possibly before you could ever speak for yourself, where God touches with promises. He said eternal life is yours because of the death and resurrection of His Son. And God meant every word of it. He always remembers His promises.

Take comfort, you who run away, and begin to see the sin that you never knew existed, even though it has existed in your unseen heart. Take comfort unrighteous, unfaithful children who don't say your prayers anymore and can't find a church that you think is convenient, empty excuses. Take comfort, children, who don't deserve the grace of God.

Take comfort, you who also cry and cower in the shadows of the ark of God's mercy. It was never your job to be perfect nor solve the riddle of sin. You couldn't fix your black heart and broken world. You didn't choose to be trapped in a cursed world. You never wanted this home to be the one your children grew to love. But there is one thing that has changed everything for everybody. It is the only thing that matters.

You have found life in God's promises, and you are kept safe in His ark.

This is a new creation right now. Christ has ushered in the eternal life that God promised from the beginning. Christ was the restart of a redeemed world, complete, with a remainder left, because the new heavens and new earth are still yet to arrive.

But right now, only one thing matters: the foolish wisdom of God, the sustaining food and drink that endures through the flood and wilderness, the answer to every lament, the One who perfectly loved through sacrifice, the child who reverses all pain, the way and the truth and the life, which is real freedom. The only thing that matters is the only solution to this cursed world: restoring the relationship of God the Father, the perfect Son, killed to atone for the punishment that you will not have to eternally endure because this punishment is too much for you to bear.

This is the only thing that matters. Even though we care, caught in the world of the curses, there is a reality of God's enduring promise. Even though there is a time that looks like death and sadness and unending famine, His hope remains. Even though we can do nothing about the curses that entangle us today, everything has already been done.

But many times, we cannot see what really matters. It is hard to hear what really matters. Our family has forgotten. Our friends never knew. Our inside and outside desire something else completely. So how do we remember who we really are? That we are remembered? That these curses are the ones drowning and dying? That this temporal world is passing? That this is the truth of everyone's story?

It doesn't look any different out there; I know. There is so much rain. There are snakes biting at your heels. You will feel lost in the wasteland of your thoughts and desires. But you have heard. And you still need to hear constantly because it will not look any different out there until the return of Christ, and the new heavens and the new earth appear. So for the mother losing her child to the unknown parts of the world, for the marriages that are falling apart, for the men that have been beaten down, for the women that have been ruled over, for the parents who have held their children as they die, for the friends that cannot understand each other and slip slowly away, for the sinners who can't stop sinning, there is still only one thing that matters for all of us: the ark, the Child, your great story of Jesus Christ.

God's Son endured the worst of the curses so that you will live. Jesus was born for this purpose: to overthrow the reign of the devil. Jesus lived perfectly to have power and dominion over the curses that did not bind Him, the King of all creation. Jesus died for this reason to satisfy the death penalty needed to restore righteousness. Jesus rose from the dead for this: to proclaim victory over sin and death and to present Himself as the first fruit of the resurrection. Jesus did all of this for you to complete your story.

Your story has been finished by Christ—happily ever after. Eternal life is already yours, today. So find the places that tell the story of who remembered you: the ark, the faith, the church, the proclamation of forgiveness, the grace and mercy of our Lord Jesus Christ. Your curse has been completely carried for you. This is the one thing that has, does, and ever will matter.

Christ Carried Your Curse Happily Ever After

Where our individual stories have ended, a bigger story still goes on. Because not only did it begin before you were, it will also continue after you. And so there is a narrative that will be here longer than you ever will. Your individual story is important because it connects you to the whole of creation. Yet the greater story is vital because it writes in the unknown pages of both your past and future.

While your greater story began at the start of the world, God's Word also tells us how this will end. When God created the heavens and the earth, He promised that all creation would be restored to the perfection of the Garden. When God's creatures tried to tell their own story, God didn't leave them all alone to perish. Even as God proclaimed curses to His creation, He promised a way to salvation in the same breath. God righteously banished the man and woman out of His perfect Garden, away from the tree of life, and separated from His Almighty presence. And finally, He promised that there will be a new heaven and a new earth that His creatures participate in right now. This book has told pieces of your story, along with every man and woman, affirming that you do also live in aching awe for what was lost once upon a curse.

Especially when our days are hard, and there is not much hope to be seen in our individual situations, there is a comfort to knowing that you are not alone with your faults. You are not alone with your failings. You are not alone with your disappointment and struggle. There is an entire universe that strives alongside you. And there is an entire universe that can somehow relate to the pain and passion that you must deal with.

Even more than that, your identity is not wrapped up in the sum of your choices, the span of your lifetime, or in your present happiness. In short, you are not simply your individual story. If this world is greater than you, if your story has already begun and has yet to end, then right now, you have begun to understand that you are a new creation.

> Therefore, if anyone is in Christ, he is a new creation. The old has passed away; behold, the new has come. (2 Corinthians 5:17)

It is here today, the new. When Christ died, was buried, and rose from the dead, the curses crumbled. Death died. The tree of life was no longer forbidden. Christ had carried the curses all the way to the tomb: the sin, the wrong, the unbelief, the disobedience, the sadness, the regret. He carried our short stories to an eternal grave before you were born. Since your story is greater than the short minutes and hours you have lived, it includes both a broken world and God's solution. It is new. It is here. It is solved by Christ.

But, yes, we still experience the curses. We operate within sin and death and failure in our everyday circumstance for now. Although your greater story is already finished, the end of the story is yet to manifest before your eyes. There will be a visible end when Christ returns, when all the dead raise, when the new earth descends. And we will all live on this earth together eternally. This is the end of the story that you certainly expect, even while we live in the comfort of its assurance right now.

> All this is from God, who through Christ reconciled us to himself and gave us the ministry of reconciliation; that is, in Christ God was reconciling the world to himself, not counting their trespasses against them, and entrusting to us the message of reconciliation. (2 Corinthians 5:18–19)

God sent His Son, Jesus Christ, to reconcile the world and you back to Him. God sent His Son to Bethlehem, to Calvary, to raise up on the third day, just as He said He would in the very beginning. *"He will crush your head, but you will bruise his heel."* Christ's story was set. Your story had been told. So right now, for you, the reign of the curse is over. You are forgiven and reconciled back to God. Christ has taken your "once upon a curse" and restores your "happily ever after."

Study Questions

Chapter 1: Own Your Curse

Read Genesis 1
    What did God create?
Read Genesis 1:31
    What did God say about His creation?
Read Genesis 3:1–5
    What did the serpent tell to man and woman?
Read Genesis 3:6–8
    What happened when man and woman believed the lies of the serpent?
Read Genesis 3:9–19
    How did the serpent's curse change God's creation?
    How did woman's curse change God's creation?
    How did man's curse change God's creation?
Read Genesis 3:20–24
    What was the changed reality for man and woman?

Reflection:
    How do you see these curses in your experience today?

Chapter 2: Lies of Freedom

Read Genesis 1:26–31
    What were man and woman created to do?
Read Genesis 2:7–20
    What was man created for?
Read Genesis 2:18–25
    What was woman created for?
Read Genesis 3:15
    What was the cursed battle between serpent and woman?
Read Romans 1:18–32
    How did the "unrighteous of men suppress the truth" of God?
Read Romans 2:1–3
    Does a judge of such unrighteousness have any escape?
Read Romans 3:10–20
    Is anyone righteous?
Read Romans 3:21–24
    What is the righteousness of God?
Read Romans 4:1–5
    What is Abraham's freedom in righteousness?
Read Romans 4:16–25
    How are we free like Abraham?
Read Romans 6:5–11
    How are you set free from sin and death?
Read Romans 7:14–8:2
    Still trapped in this body of sin and curse, what is true freedom?

Reflection:
    What does freedom from sin and death mean for your freedom today?

Chapter 3: Children Are Painful

Read Genesis 3:16
    What is the changed reality because of the woman's curse?
Read Genesis 3:9
    What did God do in response to His people's sin?
Read Genesis 3:16, 20–21
    How did God promise to save His people?
Read Genesis 4:1–8
    What is the story of the first "promised offspring"?
Read Genesis 4:9–14
    What was God's curse upon Cain?
Read Genesis 4:15
    What was God's promise to Cain?
Read Luke 2:10–18
    What is the story of this "promised offspring"?
Read Hebrews 2:14–17
    How was Jesus made like the children of God?
Read Hebrews 9:11–14 and 10:11–14
    What does the blood of Jesus do?

Reflection:
    How did the birth, life, and death of this perfect Son of God resolve the pain in childbearing?

Chapter 4: What Is Love?

Read Genesis 3:9–13
    How was the relationship changed between God and His creatures in the curse?
Read Deuteronomy 6:5–7, 13–19
    What does *love* mean to the children of Israel?
Read 2 Kings 17:13–16
    How did the children of God love the Lord?
Read Genesis 3:16
    How was the relationship between man and woman changed in the curse?
Read 1 Corinthians 13:4–8
    What is the action of love?
Read Ephesians 5:22–31
    What is the advice for men and women who struggle in the curse?
Read Ephesians 5:32
    How is this love really about Christ and His church?
Read Romans 5:8
    What does the action of love God show us?
Read John 3:16
    What is the action of love that God gave us?

Reflection:
    How does God's action love of God redefine our love?

Chapter 5: Unearned Thorns

Read Genesis 3:17–18
    What is the changed world the man has to struggle in?
Read Romans 8:21–23
    What is the cry of all creation?
Read Psalm 13
    What is the prayer of David?
Read Psalm 51
    What is the prayer of David?
Read Revelation 6:9–10
    What do even the saints who have gone before pray?
Read Luke 22:41–42
    What was the prayer of Jesus?
Read Matthew 16:24–25
    What does it mean to follow Jesus?
Read Revelation 21:1–4
    What is the promise of the new earth, after the curses have passed away?

Reflection:
    How can you pray to God your present disappointment and confident hope at the same time?

Chapter 6: More Than You Can Handle

Read Genesis 3:19
    What is the ultimate curse on the creation?

Read 1 Corinthians 10:12–13
    This is misunderstood to mean "God will not give you more than you can handle." What is the actual comfort in this verse?

Read Romans 6:23
    What is the penalty for sin? And how do we know everyone is still trapped in sin?

Read 1 Corinthians 15:20–22
    What did Christ resolve?

Read Romans 5:1–6
    What do the "justified" rejoice in?

Read 1 Kings 19:3–8
    What happened when Elijah experienced more than he could handle?

Read Romans 11:32
    What is the benefit of disobedience, suffering, and hardship?

Reflection:
    How can "more than you can handle" be a blessing from God?

Chapter 7: Wisdom, Not What You Thought

Read Genesis 3:1–5
   What was the command of God concerning the tree of knowledge?
Read Genesis 3:6–7
   What happened to the creatures when they ate from the tree of knowledge?
Read Genesis 3:22
   What was God's concern about the knowledge man and woman now possessed?
Read Genesis 3:23–24
   What is the new reality for the man and woman concerning the tree of life in a world of the curses?
Read Proverbs 3:13–18
   How is wisdom described?
Read 1 Corinthians 2:1–7
   What is the secret wisdom of God?
Read Galatians 3:10–14
   How did Christ on a "tree" redeem us from the curses?
Read 1 Peter 2:24
   How does this "tree" give us life?
Read Revelation 22:1–5
   How is the tree of life described in the new heaven and new earth?
Read Revelation 22:14
   Who has access to the tree of life once again?

Reflection:
   What is the wisdom of God?
   How does Christ restore the tree of life that had been lost in the wasteland of curses?

Chapter 8: Only One Thing Matters

Read Genesis 6:5–7
    What did God see in His cursed creation?
Read Genesis 6:17–20
    What was God's solution to the wickedness in His world?
Read Genesis 8:1
    What did God finally do?
Read Genesis 8:15–17
    How does this look like a "new creation"?
Read Genesis 9:12–17
    What is God's promise?
Read 1 Peter 3:18–22
    How does the ark correspond to baptism?
Read John 3:16
    What is God's promise?
Read Genesis 3:15
    What is the cursed battle that mankind must endure?
    What is God's promise?
Read Romans 6:3–11
    How are we united to the death and resurrection of Christ?
Read Romans 6:7–8
    What is God's promise?

Reflection:
    How do you know God's promise of life and restoration are *for you*?

Pray the Flood Prayer:

> Almighty and eternal God, according to Your strict judgment, You condemned the unbelieving world through the flood, yet according to Your great mercy You preserved believing Noah and his family, eight souls in all. You drowned hard-hearted Pharaoh and all his host in the Red Sea, yet led Your people Israel through the water on dry ground, prefiguring this washing of Your Holy Baptism. Through the Baptism in the Jordan of Your beloved Son, our Lord Jesus Christ, You sanctified and instituted all waters to be a blessed flood, and a lavish washing away of sin. We pray that You would behold (name) according to Your boundless mercy and bless him with true faith by the Holy Spirit that through this saving flood all sin in him which has been inherited from Adam and which he himself has committed since would be drowned and die. Grant that he be kept safe and secure in the holy ark of the Christian Church, being separated from the multitude of unbelievers and serving Your name at all times with a fervent spirit and a joyful hope, so that, with all believers in Your promise, he would be declared worthy of eternal life, through Jesus Christ, our Lord. Amen.

About the Author

Cindy Koch lives in Southern California with her family. Cindy earned her BA from Concordia University–Irvine, an MA in exegetical theology from Concordia Seminary–St. Louis, and is currently pursuing a PhD in Bible. She is a blog contributor to the jaggedword.com, 1517.org, thred.org, and publishes Bible studies on substack.com. Cindy speaks at women's retreats and conferences around the country. She also hosts a podcast called Family Style Theology that features roundtable conversations with children about theological topics. Find more of Cindy's writings and projects at cindykochwrites.com.

Printed in the USA
CPSIA information can be obtained
at www.ICGtesting.com
LVHW091502051124
795745LV00001B/141